The Journey In:
Creating the Life You Desire

By: Cheryl Schwartz, M.A.,CC

ISBN: 9781500298364

1. Self-Help
2. Life Coaching
3. Psychology
4. Social Work
5. Social Sciences

Cover Art: Melita Q. Schwartz
Book Graphics: Cheryl Schwartz & Taylor Ivey
Book Producer: Cheryl Schwartz
Reviewers and Copyeditors: Kellie Mitchell, Verna Lind, Melita Schwartz, Mark Schwartz, Jordana DeZeeuw Spencer, and Dan Spencer
Jacket Quotes: Rev. Dr. Dan & Dr. Jordana DeZeeuw Spencer and Tracy Puett, M.A.

Dedication

This book is dedicated to you. May you find the life you desire on this journey.

Contents

Introduction

"It is never too late to be what you might have been" (George Eliot). Taking a "journey in" to create the life you desire takes courage and support. There are many stages; many steps and stories to creating a desired life. We all possess the story of where we have been, what we are experiencing in this moment, and where we hope to go. Regardless of where you are on your "journey in," this guidebook provides you a "time in" to reflect on and create your desired story, while building tools for creating the life you desire. Open your metaphoric, or literal, toolbox; we are going to fill it!

There are many moments in life that can change your course and provide opportunity for what can be. Marcel Proust eloquently stated: "The true voyage of discovery lies not in seeking new landscapes, but in having new eyes." The *Journey In* guides you through the process of opening your eyes to the possibilities and opportunities; discovery is the outcome.

The moment in my life that changed my course (the course that led to the making of this guidebook) began on June 14, 1990 when I was working a seasonal job as a river raft guide. The summer of 1990 was an epic whitewater season in Colorado. There was an abundant snowpack that winter, creating bountiful and downright scary-fast water in most rivers. The Arkansas River, the river on which we guided, was particularly full and fast that summer. At one point during a training run, we found out that our usual section of river was the only section open to rafting that day, due to recent accidents resulting in multiple deaths because of the rough water. However, our supervisor made a go of it, even with "go at your own risk" warnings – he exclaimed "what could go wrong?"

During our first run of the day, we quickly discovered why much of the Arkansas River was closed to rafting. Our raft was sailing down mammoth rapids at speeds not experienced by any of us in the past. Whole trees were joining us on our journey! As we began to take turns guiding that morning, the first guide wrapped our boat around a large rock – the power of the water creating such an enormous force around the boat that it took us nearly an hour to break the boat free from the rock. This was a blatant reminder of the power of water and our inability to harness or control it.

The next run started with most of us feeling some trepidation and discomfort, but we went on as directed by our superior. The second guide possessed the least amount of experience on our crew and was very nervous about guiding that morning. At the top of a half-mile stretch of class 4-5 rapids was a very large rock that in prior weeks had been quite navigable. In the past, water flowed around it beautifully, creating a path of least resistance for us to follow. Today, however, this rock was barely visible and created the largest rapid on this stretch of the river. The sink hole (a wave of water coming back towards the back side of a rock) was the size of a small city (so it seemed) and the power of the water going over the rock was stronger than imaginable. For those of you who have rafted before, you probably know that you go around rocks, not over them… That is not what happened. The guide sent our raft sailing right over the top; digging the nose of the boat into the sinkhole at the backside, flipping the guide through the air off the stern right onto my head, forcing me onto the center tort (a tort is the cross-support that keeps the raft from collapsing). The raft did not completely flip, but took on so much water that I had bruising over 90% of my legs from hitting the rocks and debris in the river as I lay paralyzed, unable to move from the center tort, for the full half-mile of our journey before it was safe to pull over to the side of the river.

I knew in an instant that I was seriously injured – the fear building in me was nearly unbearable. I was experiencing numbness and tingling down my arms and into my hands, had major neck pain, and a blazing headache. To this day, I chronically experience all of those symptoms. Breaking my neck, and its lasting consequences, was the defining; pivotal moment of change that created my journey of questioning my resilience and forcing me to create a new life for myself.

I didn't have a choice but to recreate my life – everything had changed. I could no longer participate in or at the same level of activities and work that I had enjoyed. At 25 years old, a time when I felt somewhat invincible and capable of everything, I had to rediscover and ultimately redefine who I was and what I was capable of, as well as identify what would become of my life. This journey was arduous, I am not going to lie, but it was so incredibly worth it. I changed: mind, body, spirit, and emotion. This quote by Alice Mackenzie Swaim became a bit of a mantra: "Courage is not the towering oak that sees storms come and go; it is the fragile blossom that opens in the snow." There were, and still are, many blossoms, even when I least expect them. The lessons and tools I gained have been the core of my work with others for the past 25 years. I will share many of them in this guidebook.

I am a life coach, consultant, educator, and facilitator. This guidebook is a culmination of decades of work with others; from two year olds to teenagers, from college students to administrators, from wounded individuals to leaders, from teams of hardworking coworkers to couples in relationships. Nary has a story, challenge, or transition been missed. I am fortunate to have worked with amazing people, like you, who want nothing more than to live the life you desire.

This guidebook is meant to serve as a tool in your metaphoric and literal toolbox. You will find topics that range from *self-care* to *communication* to *mindfulness practices* and everything in between. This book serves as an ongoing guide that provides information, inspirational examples and stories, activities for practically applying what you have learned, and an opportunity for reflection. This guidebook is a *workbook* of sorts that you can revisit as necessary. It is sequenced and builds on itself with tools and practice. I encourage you to do each activity as you go and then go back to the activities at later dates to see if the results are different; new moments create new opportunities.

The activities in the guidebook will be noted with this symbol: . You are invited to use the space provided in the guidebook for the activities (worksheets & Journey Journal) and to capture your "story" (reflections) and "ah-ha" moments (learnings). You are also welcome to use your own special journal. Some activities require additional materials and will be noted as such. This book can be completed individually, with a partner, or as a team.

This guidebook will serve many purposes in your life. It will give you a language with action steps for moving forward. It will assist you in living a moment-to-moment intentional life of joy and passion. It will get you unstuck. It will provide context for a sometimes unclear moment. It will break down into smaller pieces that which seems large and overwhelming. It will help you become the superhero of your own story, of your own life.

Materials Needed: Playdough, Journal, and Pen

To begin your journey, I invite you to participate in an activity that will set the tone for our work together and gauge where you find yourself at the beginning of your journey towards your desire life. This activity is called: "Mold Me." Open the canister of Playdough and complete these steps:

1. Using your Playdough, mold a representation of who you think you are in this moment. For example, if I was in the room with you (meeting you for the first time) and you wanted me to know more about you, what iconic structure, character, or symbols would you mold in your Playdough to convey your message about who you are in this moment?

2. Write in your journey journal what you created, what you think and feel about it, and what ah-ha's (learnings) you discovered.

3. Now, mold with your Playdough, a representation of the "journey" you <u>want</u> to take, using this guidebook, towards your desired life.

4. Write in your journey journal what you created, what you think and feel about it, and what ah-ha's you discovered.

5. Lastly, mold with your Playdough, a representation of the <u>desired life</u> you perceive in this moment as an outcome.

6. Write in your journey journal what you created, what you think and feel about it, and what ah-ha's you discovered.

Let's begin your journey...

Introduction Journey Journal:

_____

_____

_____

_____

_____

_____

_____

_____

_____

_____

_____

_____

_____

_____

_____

_____

_____

_____

_____

_____

_____

_____

Chapter 1

A Foundation From Which to Proceed

My river rafting accident produced unmanageable pain and angst. I spent a great deal of time trying to manage day-to-day pain levels, while trying to figure out the necessary steps in the largest process I had encountered in my life to date. There were doctor's appointments, physical therapy sessions, a subsequent move back to Denver to be closer to medical care and family, and many restless days and sleepless nights from pain and fear. It was recommended I have neck fusion surgery, but approval took 10 months by workers compensation. That was the longest 10 months of my life. During that time, I utilized many Western Medicine approaches to feel better. It was not enough. I needed approaches that would address my holistic needs: calming strategies for my worrying "mind," pain management for my ailing "body," guidance and peace for my struggling "spirit," and fear management for my anxious "emotions." The rehabilitation center recommended Biofeedback Therapy as a means for physiologically calming and managing my breathing, heart rate, muscles, and ultimately my pain levels. I was attached to a few types of monitors to gauge my progress, while utilizing visualization techniques. I found this useful, if I could incorporate and address all four holistic components (mind, body, spirit, and emotion). This led me on a journey to find other forms of holistic approaches that I could do on my own outside of the rehabilitation center. I discovered and employed mindfulness meditation, guided meditation, guided visualization, breathing exercises, journaling, psychotherapy, massage therapy, and acupuncture. The combination of both Western and Eastern approaches provided some pain relief, but more than that, it created tools for my toolbox that to this day I utilize for all aspects of my life.

My journey of healing was not a pre-surgery venture – it has been a 25-year process of research, exploration, and discovery of the possibilities to remain upright and productive, to the best of my day-to-day, moment-to-moment ability. The tools I have collected over the years, and continue to discover, are the "foundation" of my existence: mind, body, spirit, and emotion. The foundation I am choosing for this guidebook is from the teachings of Mindfulness practice. Although Mindfulness finds its roots in Buddhist meditation, I am not Buddhist, but have found great passion for and self-actualization from its teachings. For our purposes, I have defined Mindfulness as: A focus on the present moment, while acknowledging and accepting one's mental/intellectual, bodily, spiritual, emotional, and soulful sensations and presence. At the center of Mindfulness is an awakening to and practice of Mindfulness Attitudes that create awareness and intention for moment-to-moment presence. Many practitioners, theorists, and writers have penned and taught abundant variations of Mindfulness Attitudes. I will do the same here from my own experience of practicing and teaching them. To achieve Mindfulness, you must quiet the mind, through meditation or other forms of focus, to discover what organically flows through and becomes present and meaningful. Being fully present in each moment takes practice, patience, and may create some discomfort. This discomfort challenges you to fully embrace all that is possible in this moment and to acquire what can be for the life you desire.

Mindfulness aficionados, such as Jon Kabat-Zinn, PhD (founding Executive Director of the Center for Mindfulness in Medicine, Health Care, and Society at the University of Massachusetts Medical School and educator in Mindfulness-Based Stress Reduction), refers to the 7 Pillars of Mindfulness Attitudes: Non-Judging, Patience, Beginners Mind, Trust, Non-Striving, Acceptance, and Letting Go in his work and publications. In exploring, practicing, and teaching Mindfulness Attitudes over the years, I have discovered many variations of Mindfulness Attitudes and also created and implemented some of my own. As the foundation for this guidebook, I have compiled 14 Mindfulness Attitudes to assist you on your journey. They include:

1. Beginners Mind
2. Suspending Judgment
3. Acceptance
4. Letting Go/Letting Be
5. Trust
6. Openness
7. Patience
8. Gratitude
9. Intention
10. Commitment
11. Non-Striving/Right-Striving
12. Curiosity
13. Authenticity
14. Equanimity

In this chapter, I will define the 14 Mindfulness Attitudes, will explain why they are important for everyday living, and will give some insight into how they can be used as you move forward throughout this guidebook and in your life. As with the other sections of this book, it is important to hold awareness of (and intention to) the Mindfulness Attitude that is calling to you in each moment. That moment, and the attitude best suited for it, will evolve and change as each moment passes. Our lives are pretty much one big continuum (or continuums). When you accept and embrace fluidity – the ability to move back and forth on your "continuum" in each moment – you will find acceptance and peace and can move forward, toward the life you desire, with greater Mindfulness.

 Materials Needed: Journal and Pen

For each Mindfulness Attitude listed below, I invite you to complete this Four-Step Mindfulness Attitude Intentions Practice activity as a strategy; a tool, for quieting the mind to gain awareness and insight. These four steps are a basic Mindfulness practice that I use personally and with clients and will serve as the beginning of a practice for you, as well. The steps to complete once you read each Mindfulness Attitude are as follows:

1. Time-In: Take a "time in" for yourself. Position yourself in comfort (lie-down on your back or sit in a comfortable chair). Close your eyes. Take a number of deep breaths with your belly rising on inhalation and lowering on exhalation. Clear your "active" thoughts to the best of your ability. Hold awareness of what you feel and what moves through you.

2. Reflection: Reflect on what you discovered in your "time in" and actively write down in your journal your thoughts about the Mindfulness Attitude in this moment.

3. Inquiry: Ask yourself some key questions about the Mindfulness Attitude. Each Mindfulness Attitude will contain Inquiry Questions for you to ponder. Write the answers in your journal.

4. Rewrite: Take time to rewrite the story you originally created about that Mindfulness Attitude and include what you now know to be true now after your time-in, reflection, and inquiry (i.e., was there a perception or assumption you held as truth that now has a different definition)?

Here are the 14 Mindfulness Attitudes I have chosen for you to examine and use as a foundation for your journey:

Beginners Mind

- Definition: Making each moment new and void of judgment of what has been; creating what can be.

- Why it is important: As you enter new moments or experiences, you can bring with you the baggage, which I will call "Mindsonite" luggage, of the past – sometimes positive and sometimes negative – that can serve your new moment, or hold you back. Either way, bringing your Mindsonite with you positions you in your new moment or experience from a place of judgment of what has been. This judgment is full of past perceptions, assumptions, lessons, behaviors, and/or stuck-ness that disallows an authentic moment now. Beginners mind is the practice of unloading your Mindsonite at the door and making each new moment a new beginning; a fresh start for what can be. My Mindsonite luggage during the process of recreating my new life after my rafting accident was the fear that I was "less than" because I couldn't be the athlete I once was. I made many assumptions about what I could and could not do and needed to seek truth to concretely know more about my limitations.

- How to do it: Unloading your Mindsonite at the door is not easy, as you can feel like you are abandoning your expertise or vital life lessons that can serve you now. In some cases, bringing your expertise and life lessons with you is important. The key to beginners mind is knowing the difference between what is useful and knowing that which holds you back. If your Mindsonite is full of judgment, lack of trust, fear, or impatience it is likely best to check it with the doorperson.

- Complete the Four-Step Mindfulness Attitude Intentions Practice (Time-In, Reflection, Inquiry, Rewrite) activity provided above in this chapter with the inclusion of these inquiry questions:

  - What are you bringing with you into this new moment that is helpful and what is hindering your process of moving forward? How can you check your Mindsonite at the door? What judgment do you feel and where is that coming from? How will you benefit from the practice of beginners mind?

Suspending Judgment

- Definition: A judgment is a negative assumption that creates false knowing. Suspending judgment of self, others, a situation, or challenges is a process of creating knowing through inquiry that will create what is true and possible.

- Why it is important: Judgment, an assumption that often turns out to be untrue and hinders your process of getting what you want, is toxic, unproductive, and results in a painful experience for you and others. Understanding the difference between negative "assumptive" judgment and positive "knowing" judgment is important. The human condition is to be suspicious of others and each situation – it is a defense mechanism that you may think keeps you safe, but can actually prevent any positive movement forward. By suspending judgment, you can come to a place of knowing and truth that naturally propels you, and your relationships, forward. I developed and managed a youth services program for eight years; working with amazing, but often "at risk" teens. Teenagers are notorious at judging others – it was often a rite of passage to do so when they were lacking esteem and self-efficacy. We created a group culture in the program of compassionate understanding which included: "Assume we are more alike than not and strive for truthful understanding." This cultural norm created a safe-zone, free of bullying, that was empowering.

- How to do it: The first step is not necessarily taken with your mouth or feet. In other words, it is important to take the necessary steps to come to awareness and find out what is true and not make assumptions, and thus judge what you "assume" or "think" is true. When faced with a person or situation about which you feel judgment (attitudes, opinions, and false truths), take steps to suspend judgment.

- Complete the Four-Step Mindfulness Attitude Intentions Practice (Time-In, Reflection, Inquiry, Rewrite) activity provided above in this chapter with the inclusion of these inquiry questions:

o Are you judging another person out of jealousy? Is fear from a past experience creating the judgment that you feel now? What purpose does judgment fulfil for you in this moment and what will the long-term effects be?

Acceptance

- Definition: A truth in this moment of feelings, thoughts, and beliefs that creates inner harmony.

- Why it is important: Mind, body, spirit, and emotion harmony creates in you the ability to be fully present for self and others and to actualize all of the possibilities. Not accepting what is real, what is truth, creates a sense of "dis-ease" that is the catalyst for a level of discomfort that at best is a process stopper and at its worse, disease and illness. I recently lost a close friend and mentor to cancer. He miraculously lived years longer than expected, which I am guessing had something to do with his amazing ability to find acceptance; an inner harmony with his diagnosis and prognosis. During his years of living with cancer, he discovered truths and beliefs about himself and about cancer that motivated him to write a book during this time. The title speaks for itself: *Letting Go: My journey to wholeness and joy living with terminal cancer* (Ward Flynn, September 2012).

- How to do it: Acceptance is the process of trusting that this moment is what it is and may not be permanent. What you know to be true about this moment may have many moving parts that are not always visible, available, or in your control. It is important to work a process of awareness and create a full picture of what this moment holds. Acceptance is difficult because it often means trusting what you don't like or what you don't know or want to be true.

- Complete the Four-Step Mindfulness Attitude Intentions Practice (Time-In, Reflection, Inquiry, Rewrite) activity provided above in this chapter with the inclusion of these inquiry questions:

    o What are the moving parts, pieces, themes, or components of what you are to accept? Can you break down what you are to accept into smaller parts? Can you assign your negotiables and non-negotiables to all of the parts of what you are accepting? What part of acceptance is about this moment and what is a longer-term-prospect?

Letting Go/Letting Be:

- Definition: A detachment that creates potential for newness. Leaving something or someone "Be" on its own; taking a pause with intention.

- Why it is important: Letting go has the power to create new possibilities that are yet to be discovered. Just "Be-ing" in this moment creates pause for what can be. There are times when you may hold on to the most dysfunctional thing in your life because it is what you know to be true; it is tangible because it has already happened. The challenge is to leap into the void of the unknown. Taking that leap opens up endless possibilities. Without that leap, you can stay in a pattern of discomfort and dysfunction that prevents a full life. I have worked on many challenge/ropes courses; activities where a participant is placed in a harness and attached to ropes while climbing 20-40 feet off the ground to accomplish the goal of, for example, walking along a horizontal pole. Imagine a horizontal utility pole attached to two vertical utilities poles the full structure looking like a football goalpost. The objective of the activity is that the participant (in harness and attached to a climbing rope) climbs up one of the vertical poles (there are metal footholds on which to stand) and then walks across the horizontal pole with nothing to hold onto. They are 30 feet off the ground and must use their own balance, and courage, to make their way across. Once across, they are lowered to the ground by the belayer (the person at the other end of the rope keeping them from falling to the ground). In my experience, the participants often freeze once they make their way up the vertical pole; holding onto that vertical pole for dear life. This pole has become their new best friend. In order to move forward with the activity, they must let go of the vertical pole, turn 180 degrees to face the horizontal pole and then begin their walk across it. The vertical pole represents "that which they 'safely' know to be true" and they don't often want to let go. The horizontal pole represents "the leap into the unknown" which is scary because they don't yet know what that experience will hold. Their perception is that they "don't possess enough balance" or the "pole might shake." This is the perfect metaphor for letting go of what we know to be true for what can be – participants found that they *did* possess the balance and courage to make it across the horizontal pole and that this leap of faith into the unknown produced a sense of accomplishment, self-reliance, and resilience they didn't know they had.

- How to do it: Letting go requires a "letting be" of what has been. Where you have been, and even where you currently find yourself, is over. That can be the good news. Even the most exciting and joyous moments are just that – moments. What comes next is to be discovered. This unknowingness can be fear producing, so careful steps are advised. It is important to note that what lies ahead is just a "moment" as well. Undo and redo are acceptable if this new moment isn't what you desire.

- Complete the Four-Step Mindfulness Attitude Intentions Practice (Time-In, Reflection, Inquiry, Rewrite) activity provided above in this chapter with the inclusion of these inquiry questions:
  - What are you holding onto? By your letting go, what can you gain? What does letting Be mean in this situation and what can be gained by doing so? Can fear be a guide for you, instead of a process stopper? What support do you have for both letting go and for your leap into the void of the unknown? What do you know to be true about the "unknown"?

<u>Trust</u>

- Definition: A relinquishing of control and opting for acceptance of what will be.
- Why it is important: Trust can be just one step behind fear as a process stopper in your life. There are many reasons why trust is challenging for most humans; likely stemming from a failure in trust that has not yet been resolved. A lack of trust can often stem from your inability to trust self. It is easier, sometimes, to project a lack of trust in self on others by holding them outside of supporting, loving, or creating synergy with you. Yes, it is true that others (people, employers, systems) can create a catastrophic failure in

trust for you, but it is often a lack of trust you can hold in self to find resolve that keeps you from forgiveness, love, and ultimately trusting again. Taking the journey to understand your challenges with trust and actively becoming trusting and trustworthy is the key to unlocking all that can be. I have spent many years facilitating team building retreats with a variety of organizations. Inevitably, trust is an issue with work-teams living in challenge and/or discourse. Creating trust, in my experience with my clients and in my own life, is largely related to accountability, communication, and consistency. Mending broken trust requires complete ownership of past actions or transgressions that created a lack of trust, collaboration in creating the solutions, and consistency of practice in each moment to build and sustain newfound trust.

- How to do it: Trusting requires trustworthiness. Trusting is a multidimensional process of working the necessary steps to heal trust with self, prior to or while, healing trust with others. It takes deep reflection, awareness, and work to get there and may need to be revisited many times. Trust building is often not a "light" task, as it can stem from years of distrust and/or catastrophic incidents in your life that take time to unravel. This "unraveling" is worth the ride. The four steps in this chapter can be used to heal a lack of trust in self and with others. It might be useful to complete the four steps with a person you want to learn to trust.

- Complete the Four-Step Mindfulness Attitude Intentions Practice (Time-In, Reflection, Inquiry, Rewrite) activity provided above in this chapter with the inclusion of these inquiry questions:
  - What or who do you distrust? What roles or responsibilities do you, and others, own in this lack of trust? What are the similarities to other trust issues you have experienced? What are your resources for healing that which holds you back? By letting go of distrust, what can you gain?

Openness

- Definition: A leaping into the void of the unknown; trusting in the best outcome of this moment.

- Why it is important: Evasiveness, reserve, and restraint hinder your ability to live a full life of love, growth, and self-actualization. Openness allows for an expression of truth in each moment; a genuine honesty that creates trust in self and others and makes the leap into the unknown an adventure of the possible. Openness does not necessarily eliminate fear, but it can help you embrace the courage and fear dance that all humans experience. Once openness is attained, the best outcome for that moment is engendered; the void becomes the new experience. When I broke my neck, I had to be open to my new set of circumstances and to all that could be gained from this stroke of bad luck. It took belief and trust in myself that I would be okay and that the best outcomes of each moment would be right for me. This was no easy task, as my faith and trust in others, and in a higher power, had been rocked (literally and figuratively). I gained openness through breaking down my life into small "moments" that I felt I could manage.

- How to do it: Openness takes a fair amount of belief and trust that you will be okay. Challenge the notion that all decisions are final; redo and undo is possible for almost all decisions you make. This alone can begin your process of letting go, letting be, and becoming open to all possibilities. Trust that if you provide due diligence and practice awareness in each individual moment, the best outcome for that moment will commence.

- Complete the Four-Step Mindfulness Attitude Intentions Practice (Time-In, Reflection, Inquiry, Rewrite) activity provided above in this chapter with the inclusion of these inquiry questions:

  o What do you need to be open to? What will openness create for your moment, experience, and/or life? What or who do you need to trust in order to be open? What is your dance with courage and fear? What outcomes are possible through your openness?

Patience

- Definition: A pause; a breathing into what is possible so the answers will come.

- Why it is important: Patience creates necessary pause to reflect, inquire, and consider what can be. Impatience can stem from your desire to control that which cannot be controlled. Right-striving will happen when you take the time to consider the angles necessary to move forward with awareness, insight, and trust. Control is a perception that other people and other outcomes are controllable. This is a perception because you don't know that to be true. How about we throw "control" out the window and try on "management" instead? Management, as opposed to control, implies your direct participation in its resolve. When managing, you are actively taking the steps to understand and address how you feel, mind, body, spirit, and emotion. Managing "me" in every moment (i.e., breathing if I am escalated) creates an understanding of others and/or the situation so patience can come. I can't help but think of my son when discussing patience. He is at an age where he is expressing his independence in every moment, often making us late everywhere we go. He is a constant reminder for me of what is important in each moment. It is more important that he learns to dress himself and that he feels the joy of that accomplishment, than me dressing him and rushing him out the door so we can be to school on time. I spend lots of time pausing and breathing and remembering the true intentions of each moment with my son.

- How to do it: As mentioned above, a reframing of control to management is necessary to find awareness and insight for the path ahead. Patience is a direct result from undergoing the process of "managing" the situation and your reactions to it.

- Complete the Four-Step Mindfulness Attitude Intentions Practice (Time-In, Reflection, Inquiry, Rewrite) activity provided above in this chapter with the inclusion of these inquiry questions:
  - What are you trying to control that has made you impatient? From where does your need for "control" stem? What can you "manage" about youself in this moment? What is there for you to gain by being patient in this moment?

Gratitude

- Definition: Appreciating, with compassion and care, yourself, others, experiences, and the world around you; sharing the gift of love, kindness, and intention.

- Why it is important: Gratitude, kindness, and love create a biological, physiological, psychological, sociological, and environmental synergy that sustains all life. Without it, we have nothing, period. All living things need to feel the energetic sustenance of gratitude, kindness, and love to thrive. There is much research in this area, from premature babies in the Neonatal Intensive Care Unit (NICU) to terminally ill patients to the plants we grow. It is also an unfortunate reality that people are more likely to give negative feedback than positive. It takes a strong sense of self-awareness, care, and compassion to provide gratitude, kindness, and love, but the return on the investment is abundant. Gratitude, kindness, and love are as much about intentions and thoughts, as actions and it all has great reward for self, others, and the world in which we live. When I was working with teenagers, I was often concerned about their resilience during the many struggles they experienced in their life. Early on in my work, I decided to give my struggling teens a special polished stone to carry with them when they felt unsafe, weak, challenged, or afraid. I told them when I gave them their stone that I had filled their stone with love, compassion, supportive energy, and gratitude. I invited them to carry their stone with them always as a reminder of the people that cared for them and those of us who were holding them with our love and gratitude. This was often all they needed to make it to a new day. Years later, I was fortunate to reunite with one of my past clients at an event. He gave me a huge hug, told me he was finishing his Ph.D. at a local university, and then he pulled his stone out of his pocket. He was still carrying it and carrying my love and gratitude for him with it. We parted with tears in our eyes from the knowing that one sentiment of gratitude could completely change a life – in this case, both of ours.

- How to do it: Gratitude, kindness, and love come in many forms. It is a simple thank you. A card with a message of gratitude. An act of kindness. Stating the words "I love you" to those you know and care about, and even those you don't know well at all. It is an intention of good over evil, positive over negative, love over hate. It is the gift of gratitude, kindness, and love for self that heals and resonates into the world. Most of all, it is unconditional – it is given with heartfelt intention without an expected return.

- Complete the Four-Step Mindfulness Attitude Intentions Practice (Time-In, Reflection, Inquiry, Rewrite) activity provided above in this chapter with the inclusion of these inquiry questions:
  - What holds you back from gratitude, kindness, and love? How can you show gratitude, kindness, and love to self? What would showing gratitude, kindness, and love to other living beings mean for you and them? What is gained when gratitude, kindness, and love is part of your thoughts, actions, and every day intentions?

Intention

- Definition: A purposeful inquiry, moment-to-moment awareness, an aim, a planning for making this moment count.
- Why it is important: Without intention, we are directionless; unable to bring about that which matters. Holding intention is not just "attention" to a specific detail or action, but a level of purpose and awareness that creates all that is possible. Intention is complete openness that allows for each moment to be the best it can be. Oneness with self and others occurs when we are in right-intention in each moment. In my work with clients, I often encourage them to ask themselves many times in a day why they are doing what they are doing and how it will serve them and others. An activity I do with them is to make a deck of "intention cards" for themselves. They set an intention for the day (or a moment), write it on a notecard or special piece of paper, put it in their pocket, and pull it out every hour to gauge their awareness of that intention in each moment; to gauge how that intention is influencing and furthering their day. Taking the time to write an intention and carrying it with you throughout the day creates purposeful inquiry and awareness that makes each moment count.

- How to do it: Understanding what your intention truly is in each moment is the key to living an intentional moment and life. It is important to break each moment down into "micro-intentions" – holding awareness for intention moment-to-moment, not an intention for a day or month or lifetime. Intentions come in all shapes and sizes. An intention can be "I am going to be with intention and hold awareness with intention in this moment." Other times, an intention is as specific as "I am going to send healing letters, thoughts, energy, and love to my ill friend." Intention with purpose, for self and others, creates a moment that counts.
- Complete the Four-Step Mindfulness Attitude Intentions Practice (Time-In, Reflection, Inquiry, Rewrite) activity provided above in this chapter with the inclusion of these inquiry questions:
  - What is your intention in this moment? Can your intention be just about this moment, as a new moment will likely call for another intention? What is a purpose, aim, or inquiry that you want to hold as intention in this moment? How will you, and others, benefit from intention?

Commitment

- Definition: A promise of connection, loyalty, respect, gratitude, trust, and that for which the moment calls.
- Why it is important: It is nearly impossible to live an intentional, mindful, purposeful life without commitment. Commitment is the glue that holds together each moment and creates opportunities for moving forward with success. It is a promise made to self and others that binds together possibilities, truths, and actions. My grandmother called it "stickyitis" – the stick-to-it-ness that helps us thrive in an unsure world with dignity and courage. My grandmother's "stickyitis" was largely about her strong religious beliefs and traditions; her commitment to *her* practice. There were times, however, that her "stickyitis" appeared to be a form of "stuckosis" – a level of commitment that doesn't allow for curiosity or openness to new things. The solution is striking a balance between commitment and openness. Commitment is that which creates trust in self and others

making this moment count and propels us (and them) into our next moment with loving kindness and intention.

- How to do it: The first step is creating the desire to want connection, loyalty, respect, gratitude, trust, and a moment that counts. Once that desire exists, committing to the intention, practice, and actions that it requires is possible. A level of trust, letting go, and patience is necessary to fully commit. Knowing that commitment is a moment-by-moment prospect that has many moving parts should create necessary openness. In other words, breaking down that which you are committing to into smaller manageable parts can assist in biting off what can be handled in each moment.

- Complete the Four-Step Mindfulness Attitude Intentions Practice (Time-In, Reflection, Inquiry, Rewrite) activity provided above in this chapter with the inclusion of these inquiry questions:

  o What are you committing to? What are the "moving parts" of this commitment? What is the purpose and possible outcomes from this commitment? What holds you back from making this commitment? Where are you experiencing "stuckosis" that may be a hindrance to moving forward? How can you move past "stuckosis" to move forward? How will you, and others, benefit from this commitment?

Non-Striving/Right-Striving

- Definition: Experiencing that for which each moment calls and that which is "right" about each moment; rather than striving outside of the current experience.

- Why it is important: In U.S. culture there is high premium placed on striving at all costs, multitasking, and stretching into extreme discomfort to get ahead. The result is a nation of unhealthy, unproductive, and underappreciated lost souls. Doing multiple tasks outside of a comfort or healthy "stretch" zone creates a level of dissonance and dis-ease that can be unproductive at best and lethal at its worst. Non-striving, or "right-striving" as I call it, is your intention to make each moment count with complete awareness and commitment. Researchers have noted severe decreases in productivity from multitasking. Not only is there a lack of efficiency and effectiveness professionally, but multitasking in your relationships create catastrophic (and often lethal) disconnect. Intention and commitment to each moment, whether meditating or working or doing homework with your kids, will create experiences that count and outcomes that are far-reaching.

- How to do it: BE HERE NOW is the Mindfulness mantra. In meditation, it means holding awareness in each moment without distraction from everything else that wants to come in. In the home, it means doing one task at a time and doing it with love and intention – sit and do homework with your kids and don't worry about the laundry (the laundry will get done, but this time with your child won't be like it is now ever again; that moment is over when it is over). At work, create an environment where completing a task before starting another task is appreciated and rewarded. Show that 100% productivity is possible when holding intention and commitment to one task at a time is actualized. It is not to say that there are some tasks that can be done simultaneously; there are those tasks. It is important to make the distinction. A way to know that distinction is to be aware of feelings of regret. Do you feel regret when you are not fully present for your children? Is there regret when a job completed is not your best?

- Complete the Four-Step Mindfulness Attitude Intentions Practice (Time-In, Reflection, Inquiry, Rewrite) activity provided above in this chapter with the inclusion of these inquiry questions:
  - Are you experiencing too many things at once that then become a distraction? What does it take for you to non-strive or right-strive? What holds you back from non-striving and/or right-striving? How will you, and others, benefit from non-striving and/or right-striving?

Curiosity

- Definition: Awareness and intention for what can be; openness to the opportunities each experience offers; a courageous sense of adventure.

- Why it is important: Life without curiosity would be uneventful and paralyzing. All living things need to move and grow and morph into the possible. A healthy curiosity stems from awareness that more is possible and intention in each moment is what creates the courage to venture in new directions. I don't know about yours, but my three cats haven't died from curiosity – in fact, it is their best trait. As I am writing this sentence, the two cats sitting on my desk in their beds (yes, I have cat beds on my rather large desk) are quite curious about what I am doing right now and they are not afraid to let me know (hence the "walking across the keyboard" they accomplished a short time ago). Like a cat, we are adventurous and desire new experiences; a new relationship, a new job, a new journey to faraway lands – it is the human condition to want to discover – bon voyage.

- How to do it: Channel your inner kitty, imagine the possible, be open to the opportunities, and courageously leap into your next adventure. Sounds doable, yes? All of the Mindfulness Attitudes discussed in this chapter will be helpful in becoming comfortable with and venturing towards curiosity.

- Complete the Four-Step Mindfulness Attitude Intentions Practice (Time-In, Reflection, Inquiry, Rewrite) activity provided above in this chapter with the inclusion of these inquiry questions:
  - What are you curious about? What steps can you take to discover the possibilities life has to offer? What do you think are your opportunities and what do you need to be open to them? How will you muster the courage to venture out on your journey?

Authenticity

- Definition: A genuine, truthful commitment to a greater good.

- Why it is important: Authenticity is the key to living a truthful and trustworthy life. Like the rest of the Mindfulness Attitudes there is both a self and other prospect when considering authenticity; you must be authentic with self in order to be truly authentic with others. This is a practice of "taking the higher road" and being of the greater good. There is a sense of freedom from that which holds you back when authenticity is your modus operandi. I worked for an organization once with a leadership team that was convinced they were trustworthy and authentic. They were the only ones that held this belief. Their actions were completely incongruent with their words, making them appear to be incompetent and unauthentic. What was really striking was their inability to see that they weren't "walking their talk" and that they were the cause of low trust and low morale in the organization. A genuine act of self-awareness and ownership of the dissonance they were causing would have begun the process of healing the challenges.

- How to do it: For starters, stop creating stories in your own head that are based on your own "perceptions" and not necessarily on what is "real" or what you know to be true. I often tell clients to put a question mark at the end of any statement they want to make about a person or a situation about which they know little. Creating questions (inquiry), to know truth, and committing to that greater good is the core of authenticity. Being consistent with words, actions, beliefs, practices, and relations is how to become the authentic hero of your own story and the genuine, truthful, authentic person in the lives of others.

- Complete the Four-Step Mindfulness Attitude Intentions Practice (Time-In, Reflection, Inquiry, Rewrite) activity provided above in this chapter with the inclusion of these inquiry questions:
    - What stories do you possess, and act on, that may be based on perception instead of what you know to be true? Where do you need to add a question mark? What is the higher road or greater good? What will be gained by your authenticity?

Equanimity

- Definition: Coming to mind, body, spirit, and emotion calmness, evenness, composure, and presence of mind.

- Why it is important: Without equanimity, you can become paralyzed with fear and become apathetic toward any opportunities remotely possible for your life. Equanimity is often seen as the culminating Mindfulness Attitude. In some ways it is. The other Mindfulness Attitudes, once achieved, can enable complete calmness and presence of mind. It is not to say that full mastery of all Mindfulness Attitudes is required for equanimity, it means that being fully engaged in each moment of mindfulness practice can bring you to a state of equanimity. Right-striving for equanimity in each moment will bring about mind, body, spirit, and emotion symbiosis. For me, equanimity is like living on a continuum – one moment I am on the calm, present side of the continuum and the next moment I am out of awareness and feeling a loss of composure. I know this continuum to be fluid – I know that by enacting my "practice" of Mindfulness Attitudes, I can get to where I need to be on my equanimity continuum. I also recognize the "gray area" between those two poles on my continuum...I can often live with, and thrive in, not being perfectly or completely in equanimity.

- How to do it: BE HERE NOW, again. Create a practice that provides opportunities to explore each of the Mindfulness Attitudes for which the moment calls. Quieting the mind and being with that which flows through you will create the calmness, evenness, composure, and presence of mind that will create endless possibilities in your life. The steps are quite clear and have been expressed throughout this chapter.

- Complete the Four-Step Mindfulness Attitude Intentions Practice (Time-In, Reflection, Inquiry, Rewrite) activity provided above in this chapter with the inclusion of these inquiry questions:
  - What is a practice in which you can engage? How can you become fully engaged in your practice? How will you know you have achieved mind, body, spirit, and emotion calmness, and does it matter? What will be gained from equanimity?

As a foundation, Mindfulness Attitudes, and the activities you just completed to better understand and implement them, are the theory, practice, and ways of being that move you towards the life you desire. This chapter is a foundation, a beginning, and is not complete. It is a chapter that you will revisit throughout your relationship with this guidebook and hopefully as an ongoing practice in your life. Use the Mindfulness Attitudes as a blueprint for your journey through the rest of this guidebook. As mentioned before, each moment is just that: a moment. Your answers to the questions in this chapter are guaranteed to evolve as you move forward on your journey – that is the good news – each Mindfulness Attitude, and mindfulness practice in general, is what you make of it and is what it needs to be in each moment.

Journey Journal

Capture your story & ah-ha's here

_____

_____

_____

_____

_____

_____

_____

_____

_____

_____

_____

_____

_____

_____

_____

_____

_____

_____

_____

_____

_____

_____

_____

_____

_____

_____

_____

_____

_____

_____

_____

_____

_____

_____

_____

_____

_____

_____

_____

_____

Chapter 2
Creating a Path of Least Resistance

In the Introduction, I told the story of my rafting accident while working on the Arkansas River in 1990. There are enough examples, metaphors, analogies, and stories about what happened that day to fill an entire book. We will concentrate on a handful here as they pertain to your journey of least resistance towards a life you desire.

A Fork in the Road (or, a rock in the river)

As you may recall in the story, there were countless signs that this was likely not the day to be on the river. There were closures, warning, and trepidation. At the proverbial fork in the road, we did not heed the signs and warnings. We took the path of least resistance with a bully supervisor instead of "resisting" his faulty decisions. We took the fork that provided an extreme place of discomfort that put all of us in danger and ended in a life-changing injury for me. Hindsight being 20/20, I can now say that we should not have gone on the river that day. Were there enough signs and were we strong enough to say "no" to what we knew was likely a challenge that wasn't worth taking? Clearly not, we didn't say no, and the outcomes were the outcomes. If faced with a similar circumstance, with what I now know about myself, my needs, and my ability to care for self, I would have said, "no."

What can you do when the fork in the road has clearly different scenarios from which to choose? Assessing and managing risk cannot be understated. Sometimes it is best to take the safest route. Sometimes the less safe fork in the road includes just enough risk management to go that route. Sometimes, not. Take a time-in to assess, manage, accept, let go, trust... Sounding like familiar Mindfulness Attitudes? I was not able to "undo" the damage from the decisions of that day, but I certainly learned about my own decision making process and that has carried me through my life. Create your own "fork-in-the-road" process and implement it when you need to.

Materials Needed: Mindfulness Fork Worksheet and Pen

Here is a worksheet called "Mindfulness Fork" that you can use to determine what a path of least resistance and a path of resistance might be for you. Pick a current decision in your journey toward your desired life and complete the worksheet.

Mindfulness Fork

Path of Least Resistance

Path of Resistance

1. Write your thoughts, ideas, and components, of what a path of least resistance would be in the space above the "path of least resistance" box following that line/fork upward.

2. Write your thoughts, ideas, and component, of what a path of resistance would be in the space above the "path of resistance" box following that line/fork upward.

3. In the center of the V (fork) write any ah-ha's, feelings, thoughts, next steps, solutions, you want to capture.

Follow your Instincts

Instinct, intuition, gut feeling, and premonition are wonderful guides and often get ignored because of peer pressure, excitement in the moment, impulsiveness, and instant gratification. What I have come to learn about myself is that I am a very intuitive person. On the day of my accident, however, my intuition was ignored…I was not going to go to work that day – something didn't feel right in me to do so. Also, I had a third interview later that afternoon for a great job for which I wanted to be prepared. My intuition was to stay home, prepare for the job interview, not push myself physically that day, and just be. I went anyway. I cannot fully explain why, but what I learned is that my intuition is strong and my resolve to care for my needs is most important.

How in touch with your intuition are you? Do you have that little voice inside you telling you what might be right-action? Do you get that feeling in the pit of your stomach when something doesn't feel quite right? All of those traits are important tactics in creating a pause for right-action – even if the next action is inaction. Right-action is a step, a direction for which the moment calls, stemming from awareness, intention, openness, curiosity, trust, acceptance, right-striving, commitment, authenticity, and equanimity. Come to awareness of what intuitive powers you possess and practice listening to them. Harnessing this power and self-control will manifest the correct decision for you in that moment.

 Materials Needed: Mindfulness Intuition Worksheet and Pen

Here is a worksheet called "Mindfulness Intuition" that you can use to become aware of your intuition and instincts. Pick a current decision in your journey toward your desired life and write what you are intuitively aware of or know to be true about that decision as it pertains to your mind, body, spirit, and emotions.

Mindfulness Intuition

MIND	BODY
SPIRIT	**EMOTION**

Stop, Listen, Respond

My co-workers and I did not stop when we knew we were in wrong-action, we did not listen to our own instincts or each other, and we did not respond to our need for risk management. Wrong-action is defined as an action that creates unhealthy or unproductive discomfort and includes negative consequences. I often work with clients on delineating between response and reaction in their everyday life and in decision making processes. A reaction is often an impulsive act or decision in a "heightened" state that likely does not serve you in that moment, and beyond. Reaction is often your sympathetic nervous system in flight, fight, or freeze creating a need to run, freeze, make rash and unrealistic decisions, waver on what is decided, treat self and others with disrespect...You get the idea. Response can occur when you intentionally and actively come to calm, if heightened, to gain full moment-to-moment awareness of and insight for the path ahead. As I mentioned in the Suspending Judgment Mindfulness Attitude section in Chapter 1, the first step is not always taken with your mouth or feet. If your first "reaction" is to "leap" out of fear, anger, frustration, or stress, it is likely best to come to calm and consider a response that is a right-action, even if inaction is what is best in that moment. It does not mean that you won't respond later, it just means that when you do respond it will be truly a response, vs. a reaction you will regret. Right-action is defined as an action that creates awareness, comfort, and positive outcome.

 Materials Needed: Journal and Pen

This activity includes steps that can assist you in learning to respond vs. react. Practice these steps when you are in a challenging situation that takes you out of calm and makes you feel reactionary on your desired life journey. Following the activity, write a reflection in your journal that includes what you have learned, any ah-ha's that you will find useful in the future, and how you can continue this practice to act in response vs. reaction:

1. Simply pause.

2. Come to awareness that you are heightened – read the signs such as labored or fast breathing, sweating, anger, frustration, resignation, or fear.

3. Take a time-in, an intentional act to address your heightened state, such as deep breathing or another stress management technique that works for you to de-escalate.

4. Consider a response in this moment to the situation – again, inaction is also an option.

5. Revisit, revise, celebrate, be in right-action, actualize mind, body, spirit, and emotion presence.

6. Capture your right-action response in your journal.

Path of Least Resistance vs. Path of Resistance

Water in a river follows a path of least resistance – it follows the easiest path that gets it where it needs to be without running into road blocks along the way. Water clears a new path of least resistance when it comes to a place that resists its natural flow. The floods in Colorado in the fall of 2013 created countless new rivers, stream beds, and drainage areas throughout the Front Range – a testament to the power of water and its ability to create least resistance.

At a challenging fork in the road, why do you follow a path of resistance? How can you position yourself on a path of least resistance and what does that path look like? Can you create a support system, family unit, or workplace culture that promotes an intentional "pause or stop" to make sure least resistance happens? These are all great questions and at a time of being in dis-ease, not easily answered. My flute teacher used to say: "practice makes perfect" or if you prefer "practice makes proficient," that is fine too. It is critical to practice with the tools in your toolbox so you can deploy them with ease when you need them most. This is one of those cases. Creating and practicing a "Least Resistance Plan" will ensure de-escalation and right-action when the time comes.

 Materials Needed: Journal and Pen

I invite you to sit and watch a river and take note of how the water goes around rocks and other debris; how it meanders downstream with little effort. Once you spend time watching a river flow, write your thoughts, feelings, and/or ah-ha's in your journal as they relate to the following questions – this will be your "Least Resistance Plan" for your desired life journey.

1. What came up for you while watching the river?

2. What metaphors or analogies can you discover?

3. What do you have in common with the river, the rocks, the debris, the flow?

4. What can you learn from the river that you didn't know before?

5. What is a path of least resistance for you now?

Honoring Your Path

In the 70's my mom had a poster in her home office that said: "life is a do-it-yourself job." Fifteen years later, she had a poster in her home office that said: "You have to learn to be your own best friend." When it comes to honoring your path, it is a do-it-yourself job and being your own best friend ensures self-care along your journey's path. Honoring your path means simply honoring you, the decisions you make, and the path you have created for and about you. My rafting accident taught me many life lessons, but the one that truly sticks with me daily is the one about honoring me. I can't undo much of what occurred that day, but I can love myself unconditionally for the path and the wondrous journey it created. I had no choice but to make decisions for myself that included a level of self-care, self-respect, and courage that I didn't know I had. It doesn't take a catastrophic incident, illness, or near-death experience to learn to honor yourself and your path. It begins with the understanding that you are human, and the human condition is that you are doing the best you can in each moment. The next step is creating plans, processes, and parachutes – the "Three P's" – for that which can be "managed". It also means creating a practice of mindfulness, stress management, fear management, anger management for the times when the three P's are not possible. Most of all, it means figuring out a way to love yourself, unconditionally!

 Materials Needed: Three P's Worksheet and Pen

This activity will assist you in identifying the Three P's for your desired life journey. The "plan" is your desired life outcome(s) as you perceive them in this moment. The "process" is the action steps you will take in this moment towards your desired life as it pertains to your plan. The "parachute" is your contingency plan if the action steps and/or the plan are unobtainable.

The Three P's

PLAN	PROCESS	PARACHUTE

Creating Support and Garnering Guidance

I am always "blown away" by how good it feels to be supported and loved through the good, the bad, and the ugly life has to offer. I often forget to ask for support, but when I do, and get it, it is an amazing experience. I have created a network of supporters, guides, and sages for myself from a holistic, mind, body, spirit, and emotion perspective. My go-to network includes friends, family, colleagues, healers, practitioners, coaches, books, research, theorists, teachers, facilitators, organizations, and anyone/anything else I can find to support me and my process. A path of least resistance is a path where you know when to "do it yourself" and when to "call in the troops."

 Materials Needed: Journal and Pen

I invite you to ponder these questions to create the support and guidance you need to create the life you desire. Write the answers to these questions in your journal.

1. When have you needed, or when do you perceive yourself needing, support the most on this journey towards your desired life?

2. Have you identified times or situations where your desired life is a do-it-yourself job?

3. What constitutes a support system for you – again, think about it holistically (mind, body, spirit, emotion, soul)?

4. Do you accept guidance readily or do you have specific ways you come to trust others?

5. How will support and guidance create a path of least resistance for you towards your desired life?

6. Identify people and resources that will be your support system.

Creating the life you desire requires awareness, planning, support, courage, and acknowledgment that a path of least resistance is the most efficient and effective way to get what you want. Working the Mindfulness Attitudes steps outlined in Chapter 1, combined with the activities in this chapter, will create right-striving in each moment that combines to actualize a desired life path. You are on your way! As you work your way through the rest of this guidebook, refer back to the outcomes of these activities as a resource and redo the activities as necessary.

Journey Journal

Capture your story & ah-ha's here

_____

_____

_____

_____

_____

_____

_____

_____

_____

_____

_____

_____

_____

_____

_____

_____

_____

_____

_____

_____

_____

_____

_____

_____

_____

_____

_____

_____

_____

_____

_____

_____

_____

_____

_____

_____

_____

Chapter 3
Law of the Possible

Law of Attraction, Learned Optimism, mind over matter. Researchers, theorists, gurus, and motivational speakers have provided endless information, and in some cases data, about how you can influence your own outcomes through positive thinking. I too believe that to be true. I also think there is a specific role you own and play in creating the life you desire. Attracting and implementing a desired outcome – a relationship, a new job, financial stability or wealth, health and wellbeing – is a mind, body, spirit, and emotion prospect. You must fully believe, and then take "right-action" to get what you want.

What exactly is "belief" in this context? Belief is mind, body, spirit, and emotion trust that someone or something is good, right, valuable, or sure. There is a level of truth-knowing that is necessary to fully believe in someone or something. As stated in earlier sections of this book, not relying on "perception" but finding out what you know to be true is important and key to realizing belief. Belief or believing is not solely outside of you – belief and believing in self is as much, if not more important. You must believe to trust, and trust is necessary to believe.

What is "right-action" you ask? As mentioned in Chapter 2, I believe right-action is a step, a direction for which the moment calls, stemming from awareness, intention, openness, curiosity, trust, acceptance, right-striving, commitment, authenticity, and equanimity. Once these Mindfulness Attitudes are realized, or at least addressed to a level of comfort, right-action can be made. Right-action is often comprised of micro-steps that lead to other right-actions. "Rome wasn't built in a day." I would even go so far as to say right-action is not necessarily a step forward or up – a side-step or back-step is sometimes necessary to move forward. A metaphor for this is rock climbing. In rock climbing, you have no control over where your next hold is placed – you can't move the perfect ledge, hold, or crack to where you want it to be in order create the forward momentum you need to reach the top. That perfect hold is often to the side of you or even below and to the left. You must go to where your next foot or handhold is to reach the summit of your desired outcome. Right-action and creating the life you desire is the same. The Mindfulness Attitudes listed above are key players (rock climbing holds) in getting you up your metaphoric (or literal) mountain.

Right-action: a step in the direction of the life you desire, and belief: mind, body, spirit, and emotion, exists when the Mindfulness Attitudes are aligned with your belief in and right-action towards what is possible. The Law of the Possible is made up of many important components working together to realize desired outcomes. We have discussed two already; belief and right-action. The next component is "intention," which is defined as: a purposeful inquiry, moment-to-moment awareness, an aim, a planning for making this moment count. As stated in Chapter 1, finding an understanding of what your intention is in each moment and breaking intentions down into manageable pieces or steps creates the awareness for aim and planning. Purposeful inquiry is not a Google search. It is a mind, body, spirit, and emotion research project, a mini-dissertation if you will, that yields enough information to trust that which is possible.

Belief, intention, and micro-right-action create your next Law of the Possible component: "optimism;" happily defined for our purposes here as: my glass is half capable; a feeling or belief that good things will happen when you are centered, aware, and mindful. Optimism is not an outcome; it is work – a job you perform in each moment to find necessary stasis that can then propel you forward. A belief in being capable comes from a place of knowing; a knowing of self, others, a situation, information, and that which is necessary to create possibility. Optimism comes when you are not mired in what has been or what has not yet happened; it is holding awareness, intention, and right-striving for all that can be. Yes, the glass can be viewed as half-full, provided that you understand your role. A great resource in the area of optimism is Martin Seligman's book: *Learned Optimism* (1998).

The last component we will discuss as a Law of the Possible is that which I call: "actions = possibilities." As mentioned, you have a specific role to play in the Law of Possible. It takes effort, not just positive thinking, to get that which you desire. That is not to say that positive thinking, affirmations, and oracles aren't useful; they certainly are. You also need to step off into the great known and unknown to find out what is possible. I believe that the actions you take in each moment create endless right-striving possibilities for what can be. Sometimes that action is not an active state, but meditating to come to awareness of right-action in the moment. Action is often truly acting on what is next.

 Materials Needed: Journal and Pen

I invite you to complete the "Actions = Possibilities" worksheet I have included here. Let's find out what possibilities are in you – THINK BIG. Simply write in the first box what actions you can take today that will create your new possibilities in the second box.

Actions = Possibilities

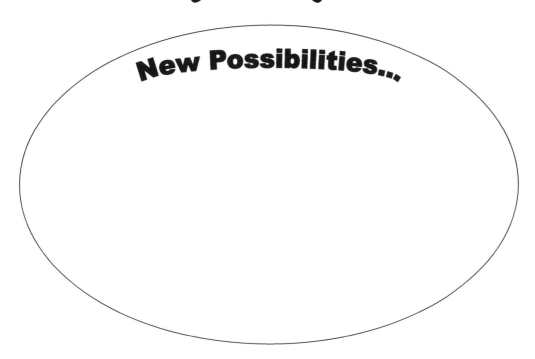

My Actions Today...

CREATES

New Possibilities...

Journey Journal

Capture your story & ah-ha's here

_____

_____

_____

_____

_____

_____

_____

_____

_____

_____

_____

_____

_____

_____

_____

_____

_____

_____

_____

_____

_____

_____

_____

_____

_____

_____

_____

_____

_____

_____

_____

_____

_____

_____

_____

_____

_____

_____

_____

_____

_____

_____

Chapter 4
Managing Fear - Creating Courage

Do you feel fear and then fear the feeling of fear? You are not alone. Everyone feels fear. In my opinion, fear is the most important emotion we possess as living beings. It is the only emotion that stops you in your tracks and makes you think about your safety, consequences, beliefs, support, and right-action. Great joy does not provide these important life-sustaining triggers. Remember back to a moment in your life when you woke up one day, looked outside at the new, shiny car in the driveway and said, "whoa, what was I thinking." Great joy in a moment may have brought that car into your literal or metaphoric driveway, but the fear after the fact is what made you check in about the right-action and consequences. It is possible to understand and appreciate fear; to use fear as a guide for what is possible and desired. Courage is the result. "When I dare to be powerful, to use my strength in the service of my vision, then it becomes less and less important whether I am afraid" (Audre Lorde).

While working on challenge/ropes courses, the vast majority of people participating in a high element, an activity 20-40 feet off the ground while wearing a rope and harness, would say that they were afraid or feeling some level of fear. My response, to their surprise, was "GOOD; we know you are human, so how would you like to proceed?" Often, they would state wanting to not go up if they hadn't yet left the ground, come down if they were already up high, or just stand there cursing. I would categorize most of these actions as "reactions" to the situation and would encourage a process of identifying "responses" or "management" strategies to decide what this moment needed. As I have mentioned earlier in the book, sometimes the next step is not taken with your feet, it could just be an exhale because you haven't done that lately. I would ask them to exhale, come to calm, hold awareness holistically (mind, body, spirit, and emotion), and identify one right-action in (just) this moment that they thought the moment called for. For some, the moment called for more breathing, for others encouragement from the people on the ground, while others needed to take a step to see what was possible. When was the last time you felt fear and allowed yourself even those quick and simple steps: exhale, come to calm, hold awareness, identify one right-action in that moment. Try it, practice it, and integrate it into your daily life to see what results are possible.

One day while out on the ropes course, I decided to try something new with a class of what I would consider "Triple A Types" – the overachiever type who thinks they can battle through any amount of challenge and fear. We were on a high ropes course element called the "pamper pole," coined for one's need for diapers due to its challenging nature. The general gist of this activity is this: you climb up a utility pole, get yourself to a standing position on top of the pole with nothing to hold onto, and stand on a round disc on top of the pole that is the size of a plate (and by the way, it rotates). You then rotate your body around to look at the beautiful mountains in the distance, make a private or public affirmation to celebrate yourself, and jump off the top. The harness and rope you are wearing catches you in the air and you are lowered back to the ground where you are met by the group with love and adoration. My Triple A's were up for the challenge and quite excited about our activity and time together. As the first person got into her harness, was tethered to her rope, donned her helmet, and began climbing the 30 foot pole, she, and the group on the ground, realized that the pole swayed a bit with each step she took. She also realized that there was wind blowing, not something she was aware of on the ground. As she reached the last foot hold before her step up to the top of the pole her heart started pounding and she stopped climbing and acknowledged (personally and publically) that she was filled with great trepidation and fear that she did not expect to feel and she felt paralyzed. I took her through the four-step process (exhale, come to calm, hold awareness, identify one right-action in the moment). She exhaled, tried to come to calm and gain awareness, but had troubles becoming aware of anything else but the fear she was feeling and experiencing. Her legs were shaking so badly that the entire pole was swaying back and forth as if a hurricane had hit the Sonoran Desert of Arizona (unlikely). I tried a new tactic, one which I had not used before. I asked the paralyzed woman on the pole to ponder what or who she loved and to say it out loud. She squeaked in a tiny, stuttering voice: "my kids, I love my kids." The second she stated whom she loved, the pole stopped swaying and she let out a huge exhale. Everyone, including me, gasped with amazement. I asked her to become aware of how she felt, holistically, and what a next right-action might be for her in this moment. She wanted to continue thinking of her kids and breathing. Then, she said she wanted to take that last step onto the disc at the top of the pole. She took that last big step and again, the pole began to shake and sway and she was clearly feeling vast amount of fear again. I asked her to think about something she loves about herself. She stated: "I love my strength and conviction," and again, her legs stopped shaking, the pole stopped swaying, and she exhaled and came to calm. I told her to remain in awareness of all that she loved, inside and outside of herself, rotate around to the mountains, and send an affirmation that would last her a lifetime. She yelled: "I love me!"

One of the greatest gifts we can give ourselves during moments of fear, challenge, or a heightened moment is the awareness; the absolute knowing, that we feel love. It is not easy to call love up to awareness and knowing during tough times, but it is the most effective and efficient way to get us to our next moment and right-action.

Materials Needed: Journal and Pen

Take time now to write in your journal what you fear and what you know to be true for yourself about love as it pertains to that fear. For example, *"I feel fear that this book won't be useful for those whom I want to help." "I love that I have stories, activities, and a journey to share."* By making a love statement about my fear, I decreased my fear by putting the intention on loving what I have to offer. I am aware in this moment that it is not my responsibility if what I write doesn't fully resonate with others. I shifted to a place of love – I am not stuck in my fear of what I don't know to be true. What I know to be true is the love I feel. What you often fear is your perception of what "may" happen, which is not "known," at least in this moment.

The aforementioned examples and steps are great for fear felt in a moment by a fear-trigger that may be actively engaging your life for a short time or in a specific moment. What do you do though with fear that is long-term or chronic? The fear of love, the fear of flying, a fear of success, a fear of failure. These fears may have been previously triggered by a specific challenging moment, like losing the love of your life or getting fired from the job you held for many years, but they are now part of you; a visceral and likely cellular part of your being. It is possible to address long-term, chronic fears by using them as a guide and moving past them to a newly desired outcome. In order to address these fears, it is important to actively work a process of identifying that which holds you back, create action steps for moving forward, and build tools to keep on track. Courage and empowerment are a result of managing the fear that holds you back from being your "best you" in each moment.

 Materials Needed: Journal and Pen

The process of managing chronic fear includes the following steps. I invite you to complete these process steps in your journal and repeat as necessary for each fear you possess:

1. Identify a chronic fear you hold and/or experience. Write it down as a "story" you are telling.
2. Close your eyes, exhale, and come to calm.
3. Identify the triggers associated with that specific chronic fear – the precipitating factor or incident that may have caused that fear to begin.
4. Close your eyes, exhale, and come to calm.
5. Hold awareness, holistically (mind, body, spirit, emotion, soul), of your thoughts, feelings, reactions as you recount the original story and the triggers.
6. Close your eyes, exhale, and come to calm.
7. Hold awareness of and write down that which you have learned and what you know you can "manage" about those fears, triggers, and feelings. Write down what you "love" about what you have learned and what you love about you.
8. Close your eyes, exhale, and come to calm.
9. Go back now and re-write the (original) story from the perspective of that which you would like to be *true* (use number 7 as a guide).
10. Close your eyes, exhale, and come to calm.

Chronic fear is often a story that gets repeated, to our detriment, and creates an inability to move forward toward the life desired. Coming to complete awareness of the fear you feel, where it came from originally and how it is continuing to play out in your current life, will allow you to revision a story that you know to be true now and desire. Chronic fear is an old story that is stored mentally, bodily, spiritually, and emotionally and can be removed through an intentional process with guidance from the Mindfulness Attitudes.

As I mentioned earlier in this chapter, courage and empowerment are a result of managing the fear that holds you back from being your "best you" in each moment. I like to think of both fear and courage as a continuum with each one at either end of the spectrum:

FEAR ———————————————————————————— **COURAGE**

Each day, and in each moment of that day, all of us experience both fear and courage and everything in between. Your emotions constantly shift on this continuum from fear to courage and from courage to fear. Sometimes you find stasis in the middle, while at other times, you need to be closer to courage to feel a sense of peace. For some, life is fully manageable while in a fear moment, because they know they will shift on that continuum to a more courageous moment again soon. The key to managing fear and becoming courageous lies in your ability to remain fluid on this continuum; to trust that it is a fluid continuum and you can shift to where you need to be. Sometimes that shift occurs with one or all of the four steps we discussed earlier: exhale, come to calm, hold awareness, and identify one right-action in that moment. Other times, a shift requires the ten-step process for long-lasting or chronic fear. Either way, shifts happen!

Journey Journal

Capture your story & ah-ha's here

_____
_____
_____
_____
_____
_____
_____
_____
_____
_____
_____
_____
_____
_____
_____
_____
_____

Chapter 5

Caring For Self: Tools for Living a "Well" Life

Self-care, stress management, time management, New Year's resolutions... Are these buzz words and goals that never get met? Are you living a life in "dis-ease" and need to be "well" in order to create the life you desire? Again, you are not alone. Dis-ease can come from many places and situations in your life and can be short lived or long-term depending on the circumstances and severity. My rafting accident in my mid-20's, when I was supposed to be "invincible," forced me to learn self-care in order to be well and thrive. Together, we will create tools for living a well life of self-care.

To begin your journey, I would like you to do a little activity. Hold out one of your arms in front of you with a straight (not bent) elbow. Make your hand into a fist. Now, squeeze your fist as hard as you can, harder, go harder, keep going as hard as you can, go, go, go, harder, harder, harder – when was the last time you exhaled? Now stop squeezing. Did you exhale at all while squeezing your fist with your arm straight out in front of you? If you did breathe, was it labored? It is likely that you held your breath or experienced labored breathing. That brief activity is a reminder of your body's response to stress. When faced with a stressor, your sympathetic nervous system is designed for flight, fight, or freeze – a systematic way to protect you in a short moment of stress or danger. This immediate response is automatic and an unconscious part of your being. In order to undo this response, you need to be intentional about breathing, coming to calm, becoming aware, and discovering right-action, as discussed in Chapter 4.

For short-term stressors, like getting cut off on the highway by another car and fearing an accident, watching your child do something dangerous at the playground, thinking the boss is coming to your desk with that look of anger, you often have the tools at hand to exhale and move through that moment with some semblance of ease. What happens though when a stressor is long-term, intense, has lasting consequences, and creates a form of dis-ease that seems to never end? What would happen if your stressor put you in the same state of being, that you felt while holding your arm out in front of you squeezing, for long periods of time? It could create a chronic state of dis-ease that could escalate from discomfort to serious consequences such as illness, depression, isolation, or despair. Some long-term, intense stressors are caused by a specific incident that was not quickly or fully resolved. Some stressors are caused by a diagnosis of illness or a tragic loss of a loved one. When you are in a long-term or chronic state of dis-ease, there is a "cycle" that is created that can keep you locked into that state of being. I call it, conveniently, the "Cycle of Dis-Ease" and it looks like this:

Cycle of Dis-Ease

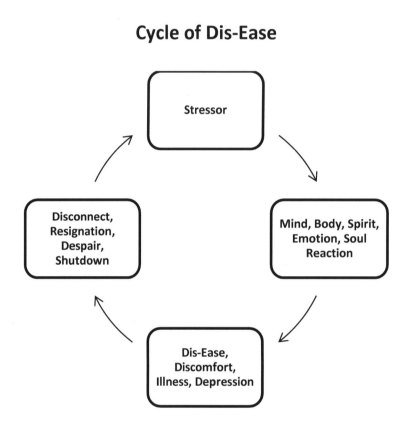

This cycle continues and creates more stress, which then creates more reactions, dis-ease, resignation, and so on. The necessary ingredients for stopping this cycle are missing. This cycle is missing the "Mindfulness Attitudes" provided in Chapter 1, the four- and/or ten-step "fear and stress processes" outlined in Chapter 4, self-care, love, and support. Already, we have outlined many processes and tools that could reverse or shut-down this cycle and create a "Cycle of Ease" as stated next:

Cycle of Ease

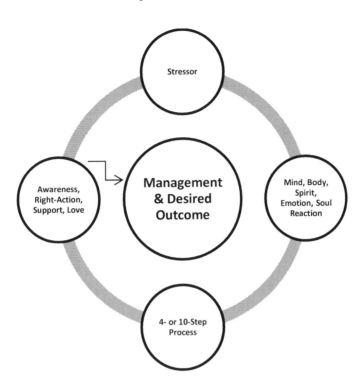

We have mainly discussed stressors caused by outside factors or circumstances. It is also important to highlight the stress you can create in your own life through fear (as discussed in Chapter 4), over-achieving, perfectionism, and complete acts of selflessness. There are many important questions to ask yourself as it pertains to these self-created stressors.

Materials Needed: Journal and Pen

Answer these questions in your journal to gain a better understanding of your self-created stressors.

1. How do you define achieving, over-achieving, and perfectionism?

2. What gains do over-achieving and perfectionism provide?

3. What stress does over-achieving and perfectionism cause?

4. How would you define "enough"?

5. If you were to create a continuum between over-achieving or perfectionism and enough, how would it be for you to live fluidly on that continuum?

6. What Mindfulness Attitudes will assist you with these self-created stressors?

7. How will your journey to creating the life you desire benefit from this understanding?

Selflessness is the act of thinking, being, and doing for others; a partner, kids, job, community, an organization or cause. Selfness is defined as thinking, being, and doing for self. I am purposely not using the word selfish, as this term has been used negatively in U.S. culture. Selfness is self-care, self-reliance, self-actualization, and self-love.

 Materials Needed: Journal and Pen

Ask yourself the following questions and write down the answers to these questions in your journal:

1. For whom, or what, are you being selfless?

2. How does being selfless feel?

3. Is being selfless at the cost of your selfness?

4. If selflessness is at the cost of selfness, when and why and how does that feel?

5. What do acts of selfness look like for you?

6. When are you being in selfness?

7. How does it feel to be in selfness?

8. Does it feel like your selfness takes away from your ability to be selfless and how does that feel?

9. Have you been able to find balance between your selflessness and selfness?

10. How will selflessness and selfness serve you on your journey to the life you desire?

Finding balance between selflessness and selfness is one of life's hardest prospects. The human condition is a desire to "put the air-mask on others before ourselves" (to use an airline metaphor). When I work with clients struggling to find this balance, as they find themselves further to the selflessness side of the continuum, I often ask one very important question: "By *you* doing, what are *they* not doing for themselves?" This could pertain to your partner, kids, job, community, or organization/cause. This line of questioning leads to rich conversation and eventually impactful solutions for finding balance. I was facilitating a team building retreat in the Sonoran Desert of Arizona one winter and was doing an activity called a Trust Walk with the group to build small work-team communication and trust. The activity pairs work-team members into dyads; one person is what I call "sensory enhanced" meaning they are wearing a bandana over their eyes and can't see, so as to engage their other senses; and the other person is their "leader". The rules of the activity are made clear – you must remain attached to each other at all times, unless I say it is okay to let go, and the only person that can talk is the sensory enhanced person. I then lead the group, in a single-file line of pairs, through the desert having the leader care for the sensory enhanced person. We climb over logs, follow narrow trails, walk along railroad ties, go under overhangs, touch wildlife, etc. As we continue on our path, I take note of how both the leader and the sensory enhanced participant are doing and how well they are caring for self and the other. I encourage the leader to stop their partner and help them breathe, if it appears they are heightened (we covered the four-step process of coming to calm prior to the activity). Half-way through the activity, we switch partner roles and continue on. Once the activity is finished, we debrief what occurred throughout the activity. The sensory enhanced person often states feeling well cared for. The leaders often states feelings of stress from the responsibility of caring so fully for the sensory enhanced person. After much dialogue about this, I share some of my observations for the group to process and then create solutions. One of my observations is the extreme way the leaders cared for their sensory enhanced partner – they were so completely selfless, they often put themselves in danger to care for the other person. Case in point, they were picking cactus quills from their legs as we were debriefing. They were willing to go off trail, walking through desert landscape, to care for the other person. We discussed what would happen to the sensory enhanced person if the leader was so selfless that they were then unable to care for the sensory enhanced person because of their complete lack of care for self. It is, for most, an innate human condition to care at the expense of self.

Doing for others has limits and boundaries. Finding balance between doing for others and doing for self creates healthy personal and professional relationships, decreases enabling, increases self-reliance, and decreases your stress. My parenting style is one example of finding this balance. I am an experiential coach, educator, and facilitator by profession and bring that into my parenting. I have provided a safe environment for my son to explore his world, his abilities, his strengths, and his challenges by simply letting him figure most things out on his own. Yes, there are times when mama needs to do it because developmentally, it is the right thing to do and/or mama needs to step in for safety. Exercising the Mindfulness Attitudes of Patience, Trust, and Letting Go however have allowed my son the opportunity to discover who he is in relation to the world around him and to create the skills necessary to find solutions, solve problems, and master his "age-appropriate" domain. This has created an opportunity for him to learn to "do for self," and in turn, equilibrates and balances my "doing it for him" for my holistic health and wellbeing. My wife's favorite example of my experiential, "letting our son do for self" style, is that when our son was a baby learning to sit up, she kept propping up pillows behind him so he wouldn't fall, but kept asking why he wasn't sitting up on his own yet. My simple answer was: "he hasn't learned to fall." I suggested she take away the pillows (he was sitting on a plush carpet with a thick play blanket under him – he was safe from all hazards). He fell over twice, with giggles each time. After two falls, he was able to sit up on his own. He needed to experience how his body worked in order to master what was needed to sit on his own. Was it easy for either of us to let him fall over? No. Was it necessary for his kinesthetic awareness, muscle development, body sensory ability, and courage? Yes. The pillows behind him were necessary when he was younger and then became enabling. I trusted my instincts and was fully aware of his development to know when to take them away. The pillows were causing us more stress than him.

 Materials Needed: By My Doing Chart and Pen

Take time now to create a "By My Doing" chart. This chart will begin the process of identifying how you can find balance between selflessness and selfness and help create an environment for others to step up to their own lives and for you to decrease the stress in yours. Once you complete the chart, share it with those listed. Here is your By My Doing chart:

By My Doing

By my doing, what are they not doing for self? (list what you do for others that they can do for self)	How does this hinder them?	How does this hinder me?	What is a solution for both of us?

Self-care, a component of stress management, is the act of creating selfness that holistically increases self-efficacy and the "well" life you desire (and you need to survive and thrive). Self-care is at its best when it includes as many of the following components as possible: adequate exercise, good nutrition, intellectual stimulation, emotional support, and spiritual practice. You get to decide what each of these components means for your life and how you want to include them. There are many practitioners; life coaches, fitness instructors, nutritionists, healthcare professionals who can help you create a self-care plan that makes the difference in your life. Your mind, body, spirit, and emotions will thank you.

Years ago, while facilitating self-care retreats, I created and facilitated the "Creating Care Model" as an example of how adding at least one thing into your busy, stressful life that you "love" can completely shift your life to a mindful, calm, and creative place. You can truly create the life you desire from a perspective and practice of "care" for self. I also diagramed for my participants an opposing model, which I termed the "Creating Depletion Model" as an example of how neglecting self-care or taking selflessness to an extreme will create chronic and harmful dis-ease. The models are provided next for your reference:

Creating "Care" Model

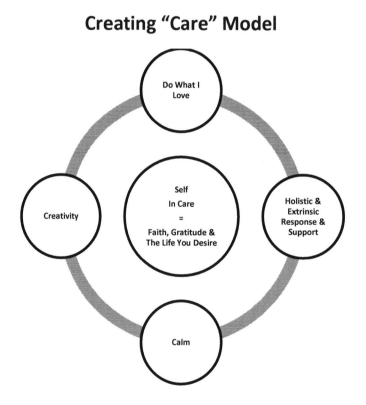

Creating "Depletion" Model

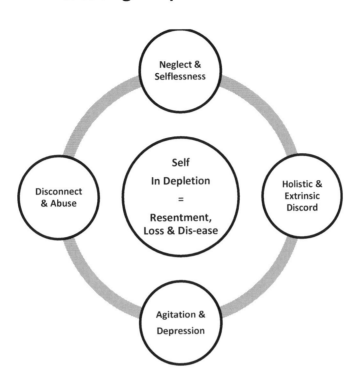

Materials Needed: Journal and Pen

Here are some questions for you to answer in your journal that will help guide you through a process of using these models for your own self-care journey:

1. Using the Creating Care and Creating Depletion models, where are you now in your life?

2. Using the Creating Care model answer the following questions:

   - What do you "love" to do?

   - How does your mind, body, spirit, emotions, and soul react when you do what you love? How do others respond to you when you do what you love?

   - What does your "calm" look/feel like?

   - What do you "create?"

3. Identify specific "love to do" activities for yourself in order to create your model of care:

Journey Journal

Capture your story & ah-ha's here

_____

_____

_____

_____

_____

_____

_____

_____

_____

_____

_____

_____

_____

_____

_____

_____

_____

_____

_____

_____

_____

_____

_____

_____

_____

_____

_____

_____

_____

_____

_____

_____

_____

_____

_____

_____

_____

_____

_____

_____

Chapter 6
Decision Making For a Desired Life Journey

I had a client recently say: "I can't make a decision to save my life!" My response: "Well, it seems you already made a decision... you are sitting in my office." Does decision making come easily for you or are you plagued by the stress of getting from point A to B? Like with most things in life, there are many components that make up decisions or a decision making process. I like to think of decision making as a process because most decisions are not just one decision – they are many small decisions or actions that make up an outcome in each moment. I taught a decision making class for four years and asked the same question to each class: "What decisions in life are truly final?" The responses were pretty similar, and when challenged, were deemed to be not completely final (i.e., buying a car – it can always be returned to the dealer or replaced later). The only decision that seemed final to each class was suicide. I would agree that for the individual that committed suicide, it was a final act. For those left behind, it was a decision that led to many other decisions and processes. If you think all decisions are "final" you put unprecedented pressure on yourself that makes that process stressful and can paralyze you from acting.

Let's think of decision making as a process of creating small actions that lead to an outcome in this moment. If you are managing the process and accepting that decisions can include a redo, undo, or a new decision making process altogether, you diminish, and even eliminate, the pressure of the "perception" of finality. The "outcome in the moment" concept is also very important in decision making. An outcome in one moment may be simply an action that leads to other actions that eventually make up a larger whole. For example, I frequently work with clients in life transition who say that they need to completely change their life or profession. This can feel huge and overwhelming for most people. As a coach, my job is to help facilitate the process of breaking that "life transition" into smaller, more manageable and realistic pieces that can be experienced as obtainable goals and actions that create the many outcomes that actualizes the life the client desires. For my clients and retreat participants, I created a "Decision Grid" to help them navigate the decision making terrain of their lives. We start with "outcome," but from the reality that outcome is only our perception of outcome in this moment. Because you are not yet at the endpoint, the outcome you state is only a guide for what is possible. Openness to that outcome being able to change and/or needing to change, following a full decision making process, is required.

Materials Needed: Decision Grid and Pen

Decision Grid

WHAT IS YOUR DESIRED OUTCOME (state it here as you perceive it in this moment – for example, "I want to have a new job by the first of the year")**:**

What are your intentions and expectations for this outcome?	What are the steps you plan to take to accomplish this outcome?
How do you plan to find balance between the needs and/or desires of others and self while actualizing this outcome?	What do you need to let go of in order to keep moving forward?

Once you complete the grid, you can move on to the next stage of decision making: creating a strategic plan. Yes, I said strategic plan (not just for corporations and organizations anymore). A strategic plan is a document that clarifies goals and provides structure for moving forward to successful completion. The strategic plan we are going to use includes: identification of specific goals; the strategy that actualizes the goals; the action plan for each goal that includes the responsible person; the outcome the goal will produce; the timeline you plan to follow for completion and implementation; the status of your progress that is updated as you go; and an evaluation of your learnings, success, or challenges. This process will: help you identify what goals are most important to you, provide a structure for right-action, keep you organized as you move forward, and give you measurable outcomes.

 Materials Needed: Journal and Pen

Here is an example of a simple, but highly useful strategic plan. Use this outline to create your strategic plan for decision making processes in creating the life you desire.

Example Goal #1: Find a new career/job

Strategy	Action Plan	Outcome	Timeline	Status	Evaluation
Garner understanding of the type of career I want to have ———— Develop a plan for seeking new employment and implement plan	I will take a career assessment to find out what careers are best for me ———— I will work with a coach to develop my career plan ———— I will implement my plan	I will have a new job/position in the career of my dreams ———— I will be fulfilled in my new position ———— I will receive just compensation for my work	Take assessment by June 1, 2014 ———— Create plan by July 1, 2014 ———— Implement Plan by July 15, 2014 ———— Complete goal by December 31, 2014	I have identified a coach that also provides assessment and will complete assessment and plan by deadlines ———— I found my dream career/job before my deadline!	The assessment provided solid information about my capabilities and career path ———— I am enjoying my new career and performing well ———— I receive just compensation for my work

Decisions don't happen in a vacuum and they almost always have some effect on other people or other things. Often, decisions require the participation of others, which adds a whole other dimension that can create stress. Being in relation to others means navigating decision making processes with others in partnership – using the tools previously mentioned in this chapter with others, will ensure equanimity in outcome. Likewise, exercising communication tools with others will inform them of what you are up to and will educate them on how to support your process and outcomes. Chapter 7 will assist you in being in relation to others as you actively make decisions.

Creating the life you desire requires a journey in decision making – that is the only way to move forward. The Mindfulness Attitudes of Openness, Trust, Commitment, Patience, Right-Striving, and Curiosity will provide necessary tools for decision making on your journey.

Journey Journal

Capture your story & ah-ha's here

_____
_____
_____
_____
_____
_____
_____
_____
_____
_____
_____
_____
_____
_____
_____
_____
_____

_____

_____

_____

_____

_____

_____

_____

_____

_____

_____

_____

_____

_____

_____

_____

_____

_____

_____

_____

Chapter 7

The Art of Being In Relation To Self and Others

How do you relate to yourself? How do you relate to others and how do they relate to you? Is communication a challenge for you? How trusting are you in self and with others? How can commitment, authenticity, and gratitude create artful relations with self and others? There is nothing more important than being in right-relation to self. There is nothing more powerful, and yet complex, than being in relationship to and with others. As a human being, you are in relation to others all the time – from personal and professional relationships – to sharing the road with other drivers and pedestrians. We are attached to others whether we like it or not. This can be both the good and the challenging news. In this chapter, we will discuss communication, trust, and commitment, authenticity, and gratitude as they pertain to self and others. Creating the life you desire means making an art out of being in relation to self and others by learning to live mindfully.

COMMUNICATION

Communication is the fine art of stating information, of truth telling – being heard – as well as being a listener; a witness to what others say. It is estimated that nonverbal communication represents two-thirds of all communication (Hogan and Stubbs. *Can't Get Through 8 Barriers to Communication*. 2003). What? How is that possible? That must mean that what you verbally express should be concise, articulate, understandable, believable, and important – not left up to chance of being understood. A communicator uses all five senses of communication broken down to these percentages: 83% sight, 11% hearing, 3% smell, 2% touch and 1% taste (Pease B. and Pease A. *The Definitive Book of Body Language*. 2004).

Materials Needed: Another Person to Whom to Communicate, Journal, and Pen

Take time now to either remember back to a recent conversation you had with someone close to you or take time now to have an intentional conversation with someone else. In that conversation, attempt to calculate the amount of times you gestured with your face, hands, eyebrows, chin, arms, legs, nose, body, shoulders, and even your "energy" or "attitude" towards what the person was/is saying or doing. Even the slightest motion or expression is a nonverbal communication. Do you frown or furrow your brow when they state something sad? Do you tilt your head and narrow your eyes when they say something confusing? Do you cross your arms when wanting to create space from that which is hard to hear? Now, calculate the amount of time you and the other person actually spend verbalizing what it is you want to say. Do you tell a story to communicate a simple truth? Do you add "fillers" such as um, like, ya'know? Do you try to fill in quiet times with your own voice, even if what you are saying doesn't contribute much to the conversation? Does your voice become loud when you are feeling angry, attacked, or agitated? Does your voice trail off at the end of sentences? Do you talk quietly when unsure of what you are saying or when you are less confident about how it might "land" with the other person? How, and what, you communicate, both verbally and nonverbally, are critical to your everyday life and for creating the life you desire. A desired life needs to be understood by others in order for you to garner the necessary support to move forward. Reflect in your journal about this activity and note any ah-ha's that will help you on your journey.

I co-teach a certificate program in experiential facilitation that includes onsite training, coaching, and a practicum. Part of the program is theoretical, but the majority is the practical application of skills and tools learned in the program. We spend significant time during the program working with participants on their communication skills as it pertains to facilitation. In order to facilitate, teach, or present, you need to be able to articulate information well, relate to your audience, promote understanding, and support the application of knowledge. Participants are given the opportunity to practice facilitation throughout the program and are given direct feedback about their verbal and nonverbal skills, their facilitation and leadership style, their ability to give information and instruction, their believability, and their resonance and engagement with others. The number one challenge facing even these seasoned professionals is the lack of congruence between what they say and how their body language presents. This creates confusion for the intended audience, depletes the message, and chips away at the presenter's credibility. During the training, and with individual coaching clients, I recommend videotaping themselves facilitating a group or talking to others as a way to fully understand how to communicate and what can be improved. When I have taped myself talking, presenting, or coaching, I notice very clear patterns or challenges to my communication. When I am nervous, lose my train of thought, am thinking out loud as opposed to having my information at hand, I say "um" frequently and my body language; my nonverbal communication, becomes more tentative. I am known for being very expressive with my hands, especially when I am excited about what I am saying or teaching. I have learned when this is a distraction for my intended audience and when it helps provide greater understanding and excitement for them.

One way to improve your communication is to simply communicate your need for feedback. Ask questions of others that will assist you in being heard and understood. I often ask my wife, colleagues, and clients if what I said was understandable. I will ask: "Did what I say make sense and/or 'land' with you?" This is my gauge for working with others and most importantly, understanding their listening, hearing, and comprehension style so we can partner in our communication. Communication is a two-way street – what is said and what is heard are equally important. There is a difference between listening and hearing – listening is the act of taking in information, whereas hearing denotes comprehension and understanding.

Materials Needed: Another Person to Whom to Communicate, Journal, and Pen

Here is an activity to do with another person to practice communication and create skills to communicate effectively together. Sit facing each other. One person is the talker and the other is the listener. The talker gets 3-5 minutes to say anything they want to the listener (set an alarm). The listener's job is to simply listen without verbal participation, response, or questions. Once the talker's time has expired, the listener recites what they heard the talker say without interruption from the talker (the talker listens to the listener). Once the listener has completed talking (2-3 minutes) the talker and listener can reflect and debrief what worked and what was challenging about this exercise, discuss any questions that came up, talk about what they heard the other person say that may or may not be what was intended, discuss both talking and listening styles, create solutions for challenges that exist, and so on. Next, do the activity again by switching roles and repeating the reflection and debrief exercise listed above. What was different the second time? What understanding did you come to about each other, your communications skills and challenges, and what solutions exist for moving your communication forward? Note your ah-ha's in your journal for future reference.

Practice makes proficient, and communication is one skill and tool that needs practice. Being proficient everyday makes for effective, efficient, and less stressful communication during the challenging times or hard conversations. Building your personal communication skills, while building effective communication with others, creates the understanding and support needed for your desired life journey and outcomes.

TRUST

Trust is a belief, an assurance that someone or something is good, honest, dependable, reliable, and credible. As a Mindfulness Attitude it is the relinquishing of control and opting for acceptance of what will be. Trust is often compromised when incongruence exists between what you know to be true and what presents as different. Human's become distrusting when there is a feeling of loss of control that creates an extreme sense of dis-ease and disconnect that doesn't appear repairable. Many trust issues can stem from conflict between a "perception" of what is real vs. what is "truth" or known. To trust requires a knowing that can only happen with truth-seeking, honesty, congruence, consistency, compassion, gratitude, letting go, and acceptance. Trust is not a given, it is earned. Trust is not just with others; you can only trust when a certain level of trust is experienced and actualized with self.

Trusting yourself is a journey of trials and tribulations that create the confidence that you can thrive through adversity, meet challenge face-to-face with certainty of positive outcome, and the ability to handle outcomes that don't go as planned. Living through a broken neck and subsequent decades of chronic pain from my rafting accident has taught me that I can trust in my resiliency – that when the going gets tough, I can find solutions to manage me and my life even if I can't control other people or other things (including barometric changes that send my pain levels through the roof). Again, that trust needed to be earned; even with myself. Skills building in the areas of solution-focused decision making, stress management, anger management, mental health competence, communication, and resiliency was necessary to trust that no matter how rocky the boat, I could come to equilibrium in right-time. Trust during challenging times, which is when you often question it the most, is a moment-to-moment prospect. Trust, as an all-encompassing part of your full being, is too large to comprehend and accept. It is important to break trust down into smaller bite-sized pieces for consumption and implementation.

 Materials Needed: Journal and Pen

Take out your journal and write down all of the things you trust about yourself. Break it down into the smallest pieces possible. For example, "I trust my ability to use humor to defuse a stressful situation." "I trust my ability to listen to hard news from others without judgment." "I trust that I won't hurt myself when I get depressed – I will call someone if I feel unsafe." "I trust the mindfulness practices I have created for myself." Now, take a look at your list; the totality of what makes up your trust in yourself. By breaking trust into smaller pieces, you can make (minor) adjustments where needed without throwing the "trust baby" out with the bathwater. You may find that you are challenged by one or two small(er) trust pieces, instead of believing that you don't fully trust yourself as a whole being. Think of it as a car, just because the brakes need to be replaced, doesn't mean you need to sell the car and buy a new one. Repair or replace the parts that need adjusting and move on.

Trusting others includes some similarities and some difference as trusting self. Like with trusting self, it is a journey and it is earned. There needs to be some proof that one can be trusted; some belief and assurance created by right-action. You can trust others when you trust yourself and you trust others when they prove trustworthiness. It is important to think of trust in others as a partnership – a ride you take together that includes both direct and scenic routes to navigate, bumps and potholes to avoid or endure, maps to co-create, and destinations experienced and hopefully enjoyed by each of you. The journey to trust must include quality and quantity of communication as described above. It must be intentional and complete with patience, gratitude, acceptance, and letting go. Trust happens when there is enough comfort to relinquish control (or at least perceived control) and concentrate on self-management. Trust includes a level of openness that allows for the possible, without fear of retribution.

Materials Needed: Another Person to Whom to Communicate, Journal, and Pen

Here are some questions for you, and those whom you want to trust, to ponder together on your journey:

1. How do you each define trust?
2. How do you each feel, mind, body, spirit, emotion, soul when you trust someone else?
3. How do you each feel, mind, body, spirit, emotion, soul when you don't trust someone else?
4. How do you each come to trust self and others?
5. Breaking down trust into small pieces, what are all of the pieces of trust you already have in each other?
6. What are the small pieces that you think might be missing?
7. How are you going to create, adjust, repair, or replace the missing pieces?

This intentional inquiry, reflection, and work will place each of you firmly on the path to trust. If a third party is needed to complete this journey, go for it. A coach, therapist, workshop, or retreat can provide the necessary tools when the challenges outweigh the solutions.

COMMITMENT

Being in relation to others takes intention and commitment on multiple levels. Defined as a promise of connection, loyalty, respect, gratitude, trust, and that for which the moment calls, commitment requires "stick-to-it-ness" for the relationship with self and others to flourish to equanimity. Commitments are like clothes; they come in all sizes and shapes and are worn for all the different occasions we experience. Each moment calls for a level of commitment that is congruent for which the right-action calls. I have committed my love and support to my wife and son, which takes great communication, trust, authenticity, and gratitude in each moment.

This form of commitment is work; it is a continuum of giving and taking in right-combination, moment-by-moment. It is worth it!

Materials Needed: Journal and Pen

Here are some questions about commitment to begin your journey towards your desired life, while being in relation to others:

1. What is a commitment that you can make to self in this moment about the journey towards your desired life?
2. What commitment to others is necessary for right-relation as it relates to your journey?
3. How do you find balance on the give and take (or selfness/selfless) continuum required by commitment?

It is vital to be specific about the commitment you are making to self and others. Blanket statements like: "I am committing to creating a new life" is a set-up for failure because it is too large, ambiguous, and doesn't include action-steps. Creating many commitments for the journey of finding a new life is more obtainable. Some examples include: "I am committing to discovering if my desire for a new life is about my career or other aspects of my life." Or, "I am committing to taking a personality or career assessment to see what my interests might be in case my new life requires a career change." Or, "I am committing to researching my top three 'fantasy' careers to see what education they require, what skills are necessary, what I can expect in pay, and how best to move into that line of work." And, "I am committing to keeping my partner apprised of my journey towards a new career and will include them in the process when necessary and appropriate."

AUTHENTICITY

True authenticity makes me want to sigh with relief. The definition speaks for itself – a genuine, truthful commitment to a greater good. When you are genuine and truthful in every moment, with self and others, a greater good is right-action and right-outcome. Authenticity is experienced in many ways: actions, language, verbal and nonverbal communication, practice, and so on. It requires consistency, commitment, ways of knowing, intuition, a walking of the talk. Authenticity begets authenticity – you cannot expect others to be authentic, if you are not authentic as well. You become authentic when you trust self and others and can let go and accept the truth of each moment; even a truth that is not what you want it to be in that moment.

My son is playing soccer, a sport near and dear to my heart as I played competitively for much of my early life. On a fine spring day recently, he decided to wear his Batman costume to soccer – not just any costume, but one that is quite realistic – a full-bodied suit with muscles built in, a cape, and cowl mask. The only hint of attending soccer… his cleats and red soccer socks poking out from under his costume. My heart beat with great joy as I watched him participating with such a sense of freedom and courage – true authenticity. His genuine ease with self clearly resonated with coaches, players, and parents as they engaged with nothing short of love and support. It occurred to me that my son's Batman soccer moment provided many lessons about authenticity:

- It is important to be the "superhero" of your own story; your own life
- Take risks to try on a new "costume" once in a while
- Try something new if the old "uniform" isn't working
- Be silly – laughing with self and others makes for a *well* life
- Ease with self creates love and support from others
- Find comfort in your own skin
- Be an individual
- Think outside the box
- There are endless opportunities to recreate yourself
- Live every moment with intention
- Authenticity comes from being genuine in each moment
- Have fun out there

Materials Needed: Journal and Pen

Take time now to write a reflection in your journal about a time when you were the authentic superhero of your life and the impact it had on you and those around you. As you move forward in creating the life you desire, how will authenticity, and its relationship to others, serve you?

GRATITUDE

"Let us be grateful to people who make us happy; they are the charming gardeners who make our souls blossom" (Marcel Proust). Gratitude, defined as: appreciating yourself, others, experiences, and the world around you with compassion and care; sharing the gift of love, kindness, and intention creates great joy for you and those around you. The outcome of gratitude is the experience of mind, body, spirit, and emotion peace.

I hold deep gratitude for you taking this journey with me through this guidebook. I am grateful you care about yourself and have chosen to create the life you desire. I appreciate the opportunity to offer this guidebook as a gift of love and intention to assist you in your journey. I am proud of you and admire your spirit.

Sharing gratitude is an important and lasting gift you give yourself and others. The energy created from gratitude, appreciation, compassion, care, love, kindness, and intention does indeed make the world a better place; one person at a time. I have shared gratitude in my personal and professional life by providing kind words of love and encouragement, simple notes, blessings, gifts, and support. For my clients, I often provide a "take home" that shows gratitude and provides hope – a polished stone for a teenager, a bead on a necklace for a retreat participant, an affirmation card or encouraging sentiment. These reminders of my gratitude often provide a necessary catalyst a client needs to take their next step to a life imagined or thrive through a challenging time.

Materials Needed: Gratitude Gifts for Self and Others

I invite you to show your gratitude to self and others now as a means for genuinely expressing heartfelt compassion, appreciation for support, and love and kindness for self and those about whom you care. Choose a means of expressing gratitude: polished stones, beads, a note on handmade paper, affirmation cards, and anything else you believe to be a special recognition of your love and appreciation. For showing gratitude to self, create an alter; a shelf or space for the special gifts you are providing yourself. Write yourself a note and/or verbally express to yourself what you are grateful for and how that gift represents that gratitude. Your Alter will be your special place of self-love and adoration. For others, provide a gift with verbal and/or written sentiments of gratitude that express the why, what, how they are special to you. Although the provision of gratitude is unconditional, it is amazing how mighty the intrinsic reward.

"He who knows others is wise; he who knows himself is enlightened" (Lao-Tzu). As you have witnessed in this chapter, the journey to a life desired is often a paradox of processes that include work for and on self and work with and for others. Answering the questions, and completing the exercises this chapter provides, as a solo activity and with those to whom you are in relation will ensure communication, trust, and commitment, authenticity, and gratitude for a successful journey and artful relations to self and others.

Journey Journal

Capture your story & ah-ha's here

_____

_____

_____

_____

_____

_____

_____

_____

_____

_____

_____

_____

_____

_____

_____

_____

_____

_____

_____

_____

_____

_____

_____

_____

_____

_____

_____

_____

_____

_____

_____

_____

_____

_____

_____

_____

_____

_____

Chapter 8

Mindful Leadership and Followership

Your journey to the life you desire may include both leadership and followership. This chapter illustrates the ways in which leadership and followership can create resonance and dissonance on that journey.

"There goes my people. I must follow them, for I am their leader" (Mahatma Gandhi). The true measure of one's ability to lead – be it a CEO of a major corporation, a parent, or sage is to truly be present with and garner full understanding of those with whom you lead. A leader is a partner who works in tandem for the greater good of each individual, the outcomes of the moment, and the wellbeing of the world. According to Thich Nhat Hanh, "the most precious gift we can offer others is our presence. When mindfulness embraces those we love, they bloom like flowers." The 14 Mindfulness Attitudes we have discussed create the safe environment for employees, children, and community to step up to being their best them for which each moment requires, making leadership and followership one in the same.

I have worked for and with many leaders over the decades and have experienced some of the most retribution-based and depleting work environments one can endure. I have watched individuals and teams in leadership positions use their power for their own agenda and self-gain; at the expense of other people and organizational goals and outcomes. I have witnessed and have been a victim of leaders who feel so threatened by the competence of others that they sabotage any morale and gain possible. I have also seen good, hardworking people promoted to leadership without being given the skills and tools to succeed in their leadership position and thus failed miserably. Time and time again, corporations and organizations provide little or no transition or succession planning and expect leaders to shine, productivity to increase, morale to soar, and loyalty to reign. They are wrong.

Leadership and followership are roles and responsibilities that require some innate and some learned skills in human relations, empowerment, motivation, intuition, and ways of knowing. Just because someone is thriving at their current position doesn't automatically mean that they possess the wherewithal to lead others in mastery of skills or manage of others outside of their current level of work. Some people are equipped to lead and manage, while some are not. The same can be said for parenting...A trip to the grocery store, witnessing retributional and disempowering parenting, is a reminder that a "license" to parent that includes training and a test might be beneficial for the health and wellbeing of children.

Becoming a mindful leader requires personal understanding of and practice in the 14 Mindfulness Attitudes. It also requires exercising these attitudes and practices in the workplace. Imagine a mindful workplace community where patience, commitment, intention, openness, and gratitude are the culture that fosters a productive work environment; where employees and leaders feel empowered, supported, and loyal. This workplace does exist and can happen for you.

 Materials Needed: Journal and Pen

If creating the life you desire includes being a "mindful leader" and "creating a mindful workplace community," here are the steps you can take:

1. Learn, understand, practice, and integrate the 14 Mindfulness Attitudes in your own life.

2. Work collaboratively with your team, company, or organization to also learn, understand, and practice the 14 Mindfulness Attitudes. Include a space and time for practice in the workplace during work hours and encourage practice during breaks.

3. Create a plan with your team, company, or organization for implementing the 14 Mindfulness Attitudes as a "culture" of the organization. Include a mission and vision statement that describes this culture.

4. Work with a trained consultant to create and implement mindfulness practices as specific tools for communication, group cohesion, trust building, productivity, safe environment, morale enhancement, and more.

Note: I co-created a program called "Creating a Mindful Workplace Community" and co-facilitate this process with companies and organizations. Let me know how I can support your team!

Followership is just as important as leadership. The perception is that followers are not leaders; which according to Gandhi isn't true. I worked with adjudicated youth years ago providing workshops and support groups to help them feel more empowered without taking power from others. Many young people with whom I worked were incarcerated for gang behavior that turned violent and sometimes deadly. We had rich conversations, as you can imagine, about power – what led them to want to have power and control over others and what they can do now to manage their lives so they don't need power and control to survive and thrive. Some were leaders in their respective gangs and some were considered followers. In discussing the role of followers in their gang, they came to realize that their leadership in their gang either stemmed from or currently consisted of followership. They were disempowered in their lives and became enthusiastic, ambitious, self-reliant members of the gang (this is the definition of followership). Through this enthusiasm, their status was often elevated to some form of leadership, but the ethos and practice of their new role was likely their perception of what they knew to be true about power and control – taking power from others to feel more powerful. Without followers, there are no leaders. Without effective leadership that empowers followers, there cannot be productivity and outcome. Companies and organizations can at times operate like gangs. There can often be bullying to get ahead, retribution for failure or success, and the perception of and need for power and control creates unsafe work environments. Creating a workplace ethic of and culture in "collaborative leadership" ensures the safety, productivity, care, and compassion necessary for collective right-action and success.

Collaborative leadership is the shared responsibility of all stakeholders to create, implement, and attain goals and outcomes. There may be a "visible" leader or facilitator keeping the team moving, but there is shared accountability for the success and failure of the outcomes. A mindful workplace environment is one that promotes collaborative leadership, celebrates individual and team contributions, values input and guidance from all members, actively values empowerment and embodies morale, and creates a sense of belonging and loyalty to team and outcome. It is a place for productive candor and "right-striving" in harmony. It is the place you want to be your best you!

Parenting and partnering with a loved one can take on many of the same attributes as leadership and followership. All of the same issues and rules apply, as stated above. Controlling others is often the result of feeling out of control or disempowered in your own life. Recognizing this is critical for the health and wellbeing of you, your partner, and your children. I often hear couples and parents say how much they wish the others in their household would do what they want; it would be so much easier. I like to challenge that notion – is it really easier imposing your agenda and having to face retaliation from everyone else? What would happen if a collaborative family leadership, decision making, and/or rule process was activated? Don't you think everyone would have more buy-in, ownership, responsibility, and accountability for the outcomes? Kids need to learn how to make decisions at an early age so they can do so later in life when you are not with them. It is also important to build trust with kids early on so they are more likely to share with you if/when they get into trouble or need assistance. I am always a little surprised when parents wonder in amazement why their kids don't talk about their day-to-day experiences or a problem until it is too late. There should be little surprise about this if you have not actively been there for your children without judgment and with unconditional love. It is never too late to create the relationships you want with loved ones – use the activities and information in this book to create the family unit you desire.

 Materials Needed: Journal and Pen

I invite you to write a reflection in your journal on the learnings or ah-ha's you discovered while reading this chapter. Here are some reflection questions for you to consider:

1. What style of *leadership* have you possessed in the past and what did you learn in this chapter that might make it different?

2. What style of *followership* have you possessed in the past and what did you learn in this chapter that might make it different?

3. How does leadership and followership pertain to you in creating the life you desire?

4. What challenges do you perceive or know to be true about leadership and followership in your life (you, your partner, your kids, and your supervisor) and what solutions exist to manage these challenges?

5. What learnings or ah-ha's came up for you as you read this chapter?

6. What learnings or ah-ha's do you plan to explore and implement as you move forward on your journey?

Journey Journal

Capture your story & ah-ha's here

_____

_____

_____

_____

_____

_____

_____

_____

_____

_____

_____

_____

_____

_____

_____

_____

_____

Chapter 9
Thriving With Chronic Conditions

Living with mental, physical, spiritual, and emotional chronic conditions that cause pain, discomfort, "stuck-ness", and what feels like an end to the life you desire doesn't need to be the endpoint. It is the beginning of creating a life of possibilities that you may not know exists. If you experience chronic pain, illness, depression, fear, addiction, stuck-ness, or any other chronic condition that keeps you from being your best you, let's strive to understand the chronic condition you experience, create and implement a management process and plan that works for you, and discover what a desired life can be for you. There are lessons and ah-ha's in this chapter for everyone – we can all get "stuck" at some point in unhealthy patterns that this chapter will address.

One of the greatest, most intense and challenging journeys of my life was breaking my neck and the subsequent chronic pain it caused. I am in pain 24-hours a day from the original accident, from the now broken and inoperable fusion remaining in my neck, and from other damage the fusion has caused. I don't talk about it much, but it is a reality for me in every moment of every day. Many people in my life are surprised to hear I am in so much pain – I hide it well. I don't discuss my pain much because I learned a long time ago that others don't often have the ability to understand or even fathom chronic pain. I had a doctor tell me once, "I don't live in your body and can't perceive the pain you feel, so I will believe what you tell me and we will work from there." What a gift of understanding and trust. Also, there is a certain "mental edge" I need to keep in order to thrive each day – incessantly talking about being in pain creates a stuck-ness ("stuckosis") that holds me back from moving forward and is not how I want to live my life. Chronic pain is a part of my life, but it does not define who I am.

After my accident, I had no choice but to go on a journey to figure out a new path for my life. I could no longer do the things I loved, I didn't have the same coping skills that helped me through the first 25 years of my life, and my work options were changing without my consent or desire. In order to survive, I would have to learn to thrive under a new set of circumstances. I have now lived with chronic pain for almost 25 years – half of my life. I have worked hard to not only thrive in my new life, but have also worked with others to do so.

The journey to thriving is about understanding your chronic condition in each moment. As with most things, chronic conditions continue to constantly evolve and change. Management of chronic conditions is a 24-hour a day prospect – what works one day to manage most conditions doesn't work the next. There are many uncontrollable impacts on day-to-day chronic conditions, including: stress, living outside of your capacity, environmental or weather changes, family or work demands, household chores…Some days, just being alive is challenging. Living with chronic conditions is often like living in a hamster wheel – you have to figure out ways to make that wheel go, go, go effectively and efficiently and stop it when it needs to be stopped. You will discover how to do both in this chapter.

Like fear, chronic conditions can serve as a guide for gaining awareness of and creating solutions for living a more fulfilling and desired life. There is often "cause" behind the condition, or subsequent chronic issues experienced now, that must be understood in order to move forward. Let's take a journey to find out more about what conditions you experience, why you experience those conditions, and what solutions may be useful in managing the conditions you experience.

 Materials Needed: My So Called Conditional Life Worksheet and Pen

Here is a worksheet, called: "My So Called Conditional Life" to assist you in understanding what conditions you feel, where those conditions came from, and possible solutions to consider in managing them.

My So Called Conditional Life

The "condition(s)" I feel is:	I believe the condition started when:	I think a possible solution to help move me toward managing this condition is:

In working with clients living with chronic conditions, and in my own experience, I discovered that there is a cyclical effect to living with chronic conditions. You can find yourself in (acute) chronic condition, which then creates distress, which then creates depression or anxiety, which then creates dis-ease, which then creates greater chronic "stuckosis". It looks something like this:

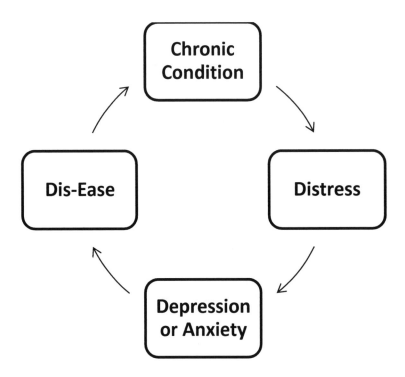

In order to break this destructive cycle, you must create solutions that change the course of the downward spiral. Solutions come in many packages and from many resources. Each chronic condition carries with it possible solutions and practitioners that can help you discover the magic fit for you. Here are some ideas that I have discovered for myself and my clients:

1. Breathing
   a. Diaphragmatic breathing (deep belly breaths.)
   b. Emergency breathing to quickly bring down heart and respiration rate – concentrate on exhale by counting the seconds of each one.
   c. Breathing awareness, deep breathing, relaxing sigh, complete natural breathing, purifying breath, nose breathing, etc.

2. <u>Meditation</u> – Focusing on one thing at a time/moment-to-moment awareness.
    a. Mantra – Select a word or syllable that speaks to you (i.e., "OM") and repeat it to yourself silently and/or as a verbal chant.
    b. Breath Counting – Silently count the seconds of each inhale and exhale.
    c. Gazing – Fix your gaze on an object without thinking about it in words. Trace it with your eyes and notice its shape, size, color, texture, etc.
    d. Guided – Scripted meditation provided by a person or tape.
    e. Thought Stopping – Letting go of thoughts as you concentrate on simply breathing.
    f. Releasing Muscular Tension – Squeeze/tighten muscle groups and then release.

3. <u>Visualization</u>
    a. Receptive – Relax, empty mind, sketch a scene (i.e., walking on a beach), ask a question (i.e., why can't I relax?), and let the answer come to your consciousness.
    b. Programmed – Create an image or scene and include an abundance of sight, smell, taste, and sound (i.e., goal you want to complete like a marathon.)
    c. Guided – Visualize a scene in detail and then let the subconscious take the scene wherever it wants to go. Guided visualizations are often scripted, self-created, and/or provided by a person/tape.

4. <u>Progressive Relaxation & Releasing Muscular Tension</u> – Each muscle/muscle group is tensed (individually) for 5-8 seconds and then relaxed for 20-30 seconds. It is helpful to travel from head to toes and toes to head throughout the body.

5. <u>Relaxation Tapes</u> – There are many tapes available for use in chronic condition relaxation and stress management. You can also make your own tape using many of the techniques listed above, writing your own script, or using a script created by someone else. It is often useful to listen to your own voice as both metaphor and practice for finding "your" calm and stress/distress reduction.

6. <u>Bio Feedback</u> – Is the use of machines such as an Electromyogram (EMG) that monitors skeletal muscle tension, a Thermograph that measures minute fluctuations in body temperature, a Galvanic Skin Response (GSR) that measures the electrical conductance or electrical potential the skin, an Electroencephalogram (EEG) that monitors brain waves, and a Heart Rate Monitor that measures beats-per-minute. These machines can be used for developing techniques that work for specific areas in the body. An added feature is that they give instant feedback about the effectiveness of your stress and chronic condition reduction techniques.

7. <u>HeartMath</u> – Is the use of HeartMath's emWave technology to measure stress and the effect of emotions through the beat-to-beat changes in our heart rate, called Heart Rate Variability. The HeartMath System offers both technology and training options to help you harness the power of your heart rhythms to manage your emotions. Doing this

reduces your stress, improves your health, your ability to focus, to communicate better, be more creative, as well as more balanced in your interactions, which in turn improves relationships.

8. <u>Therapeutic Interventions</u> – There are countless Eastern and Western medical, therapeutic interventions to address all chronic conditions. Work with reputable healthcare providers to identify the best fit for you and your condition. Some interventions include: massage therapy, myo therapy, acupuncture, Chinese medicine, herbal medicine, psychotherapy, EMDR, physical therapy, postural realignment, chiropractic interventions, injections, etc.

9. <u>Nutrition</u> – It is estimated that human's need 40-60 nutrients a day to stay healthy and prevent chronic/sub-clinical malnutrition. When you are stressed or in distress, your need for some nutrients increases (such as calcium and B vitamins). A poor diet can contribute to your bodies poor reaction to distress/stress (i.e., inability of body to clear out lactic acid from muscles) and to an increase in fatigue, anxiety, irritability, sleeplessness, and poor concentration – which of course can lead to more distress/stress. The eleven steps to good nutrition include: Eating a variety of food, maintain ideal body weight, balance fat intake, eat more whole foods, avoid sugar, avoid sodium, avoid alcohol, avoid caffeine, take vitamin and mineral supplements, eat frequent/calm meals, and avoid known food allergy and/or emotional response triggers. Many foods can cause inflammation in the body and trigger negative responses for your condition. Discussing nutrition with your healthcare practitioner or a trained nutritionist will identify right-action for your condition.

10. <u>Exercise</u> – Find a balance of exercise that works you holistically – mind, body, spirit, and emotion. This should/could include: Aerobic exercise, low intensity exercise (calisthenics, isotonics, isometrics), muscle strengthening, muscle stretching, abdominal exercises, weight baring exercise, core strength (i.e., pilates), body/spirit connection (i.e., yoga), and exercises that help to improve/restore balance.

11. <u>Coping Skills Training</u> – Includes: Relaxation techniques, creating a stressful event hierarchy, developing relaxation techniques specific to your hierarchy, and creating stress coping thoughts that reframe stressful events.

12. <u>Assertiveness Training</u> – Includes: Interpersonal skills training, understanding and reframing of "problem scenes," developing "scripts" for problem areas/scenes, affirmations, body language, listening/speaking skills, avoiding manipulation, negotiable/non-negotiable collaboration, compromise, solution-focused decision making, etc.

13. <u>Time-Management</u> – Develop the skills for addressing the symptoms of "poor" time-management that cause distress/stress. Symptoms can include: Rushing, vacillating between alternatives, fatigue/listlessness, slack hours of non-productive activity, missed

deadlines, insufficient time for self-care/rest and personal relationships, having to do what you don't like/want to do most of the time, and the sense of being/feeling overwhelmed by the demands and details.

    a. Creating an "organizational chart" of major tasks and the subsequent tasks to be completed. Develop an action plan from the chart by starting at the bottom and working your way up to the intended goal/outcome.

    b. Break tasks into smaller/more manageable pieces.

    c. Developing time-lines.

    d. Understanding and communicating roles, responsibilities, expectations, desired outcomes, time-lines, etc.

    e. Setting priorities.

    f. Creating and updating "to do" lists based on priority.

    g. Realize that work/life is about the "journey" not the "destination." When we concentrate on mastering the moment, the outcomes will happen – trust, accept, let go!

14. <u>Job Stress Management</u> – We spend approximately one-third of our life working. It is important that we enjoy what we do, keep a balance of personal and professional life, know what is expected of us, set boundaries, communicate our needs, and develop a work-plan that is built for success. The time management techniques listed above will be useful for handling job stress.

 Materials Needed: Reverse Cycle Worksheet and Pen

I created a worksheet for my clients and me, called "Reverse Cycle" to gain awareness of and create solutions for the cyclical nature of chronic conditions. I have included it here for you to try:

Reverse Cycle

This activity will help you identify both your "chronic condition cycle" and the "solutions" for stopping the cycle at critical stages of its progression.

First Step: Using the circle below, write in your "chronic condition cycle" by answering the following questions in the boxes provide (clock analogy – 12:00 represents both the start and end point of your cycle): What begins your condition cycle (i.e., 12:00 – neck pain, fibromyalgia, fear, diabetes, depression, etc.)? What happens next because of your condition (i.e., 3:00 –

lack of exercise, poor diet, decrease in activities of daily living, etc.)? What happens next because of the 3:00 items (i.e., 6:00 – lack of sleep, poor energy level, etc.)? What happens next because of the 6:00 items (i.e., 9:00 – depression, anxiety, substance use/abuse, etc.)? What happens as you reach 12:00 again (i.e., 12:00 – more/elevated pain, other health challenges, greater distress/dis-ease, etc.)?

Second Step: Using the same circle, identify solutions for each point on your cycle to address and "end" that challenging point/issue. An example of a solution could be: incorporate meditation, breathing exercises, and/or stress management techniques at 4:00, when the first sign of decreased energy is beginning. Write in your journal how the inclusion of solutions will change your cycle and what can be gained for doing so.

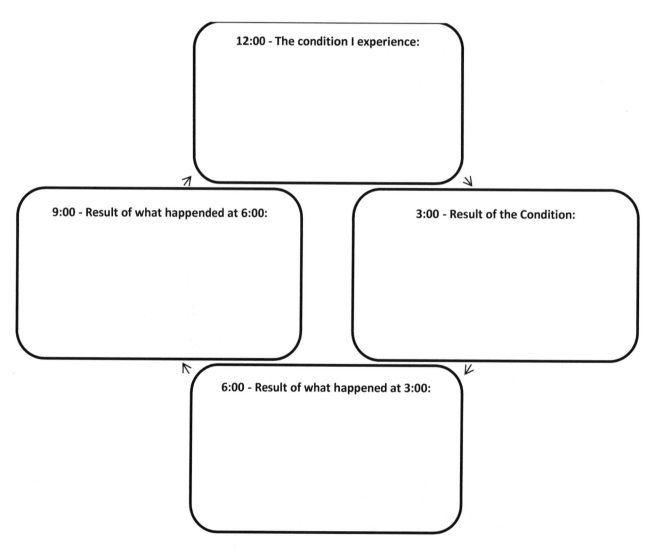

It can feel very disempowering living with chronic conditions. There are many unknowns and it often feels like you can't control what it is you want to control. A spiral into depression occurs when you try to control what you can't control and then feel frustrated with a sense of resulting failure. I have previously discussed the difference between control and management in this guidebook and advise reviewing that information with the lens of "condition management" in mind. You can't often control your chronic condition, but you can manage many aspects of it. Here are some steps to managing chronic conditions:

1. Do the research necessary to fully understand what causes your chronic condition. First and foremost, discuss your specific condition with your healthcare, mental health, or life coach practitioner. Research books, articles, medical journals, websites, and blogs about your condition. Interview a specialist in this area of practice to better understand their take on the condition. Discuss your condition with others experiencing similar issues.

2. Take the necessary steps to understand your chronic condition components and cycles using the worksheets provided in this chapter. Gaining awareness of what causes your condition, and finding solutions to address it, is necessary for the management of it.

3. Create solutions for managing your chronic condition and do them!

4. Create a partnership with your healthcare provider in the management of your chronic condition. They want to help you and are usually open to dialogue about the possibilities.

5. Be organized for appointments with your practitioners to maximize your visit. For example, I provide a memo to my pain specialist every time we meet that includes: A general update of my life and management to date, my overall pain levels at the time of the appointment (or experienced since my last visit), a list of current medications I am taking and a summary of their use, a list of specific pain issues and the solutions or treatments I am doing for them, a summary list of treatments in process and that currently work for me, and next steps that I am wanting to discuss with my doctor and/or see happen as an outcome of my visit. This ensures that you are giving a thorough accounting of your issues and needs, it helps you advocate for what you need, and it creates a clear record for you and your practitioner to document your issues and

progress.

6. Create a mindfulness, stress management, and/or depression management practice.

7. Compile resources and tools/skills that help you manage your condition and also manage the emotions that come with it.

8. Have a check-in system for yourself that is holistic: mind, body, spirit, and emotion, as they are all affected by chronic conditions.

You can recreate a life you desire despite (or even in spite) of your chronic condition. The 14 Mindfulness Attitudes are helpful for moving forward, as are the other chapters in this book.

 Materials Needed: I Want Worksheet and Pen

Here is a worksheet, called "I Want" for you to use in imagining what can be, as you move towards a desired life and the support you will need in getting there:

I WANT!

An activity to determine what you need in order to <u>manage</u> your chronic condition and create the life you desire! Follow these instructions to begin your journey:

1. <u>**Want**</u> – List what you <u>want/need</u> to manage your chronic condition (as it relates to the items listed in column one.)
2. <u>**Will**</u> – List what you <u>will need</u> in order to get what you "want" (as it relates to the items listed in column one.)
3. <u>**Sabotage**</u> – List what could possibly <u>hinder</u> the process of getting what you "want" (as it relates to the items listed in column one.)
4. <u>**Gain**</u> – List what could be gained or achieved by getting what you "want" (as it relates to the items listed in column one.)

From:	I Want…	I Will Need…	Sabotage…	I Will Gain…
From Me…				
From Family…				
From Friends…				
From Work…				
From Medical Provider…				
Other:				
Other:				
Other:				
Other:				

Journey Journal

Capture your story & ah-ha's here

_____

_____

_____

_____

_____

_____

_____

_____

_____

_____

_____

_____

_____

_____

_____

_____

_____

_____

_____

_____

_____

_____

_____

_____

_____

_____

_____

_____

_____

_____

_____

_____

_____

_____

_____

_____

Chapter 10
Getting From Here to the Life You Desire

We are nearing the end of our journey together in this guidebook for creating the life you desire. You have read information, participated in activities, created tools and skills, reflected on what you have learned, and noted ah-ha moments that will guide you, as you move forward. Now, it is time to bring it all together; package it up for what is possible and for what is next on your journey. This may be an end point – transition complete – or it could be just the beginning of what is to come. Either way, living a mindful and intentional process begets right-action and right-outcome.

Materials Needed: Journal and Pen

I invite you to take time now to review the work you have done in this guidebook and in your journal. Hold awareness of your ah-ha moments; the learnings that propel you forward, while answering questions of the past. Note your progress and also identify where you got stuck. Mindfully store that information where it needs to go, without judgment, or simply let go of what you can accept.

Materials Needed: Package of Sticky Notes, Two Pens of Different Colors, And a Fairly Long Space without Hindrances – A Hallway Is Perfect

Once your review is complete, I call you to complete this activity to help put your journey or transition into greater prospective. This activity is called "Transition Walk". Ready? Okay, here we go.

1. First, I would like you to stand at one end of your hallway with your sticky note pad and one of your pens in hand.

2. I want you to create a path using the sticky notes and pen that represents your past, where you are now, and where you desire to be. <u>This is a "free association" activity – you will simply write what comes to mind as you are walking down the hallway placing</u>

each sticky note in a line down the hallway. Write only one thought, concept, or idea per sticky note. Again, start thinking of where you have been and transition your thoughts towards where you want to be, naturally and organically, as you walk.

3. Once you have completed your line of sticky notes, go back and read them again – don't pick them up or make any changes to them – just simply take it in. Did you "free associate" content that you didn't realize you had in you or didn't capture earlier in our work together? Do you see a progression from where you were to where you want to be?

4. Now, number your sticky notes, from the beginning where you started to the end, so they stay in chronological order.

5. With your second pen of a different color, go back through each sticky note and write notes to yourself about the following:

   a. Is this a likely step in the progression for getting you where you want to go and if so how will you use it and if not, can it be discarded?

   b. Are solutions and/or resources necessary to make this step happen and if so note it down?

   c. What Mindfulness Attitude will assist you in moving each step forward?

   d. Was the last sticky note (or the last few) an outcome(s) you would like to see for your desired life? If so, what is your next step? If not, can you identify a next step or outcome now (keeping in mind these are outcomes as you perceive them now as we discussed in previous chapters).

6. Now, pick up your sticky notes in order from start to finish for our next activity.

 Materials Needed: Journal and Pen

Using the strategic plan outline provided in Chapter 6 on Decision Making take the outcomes of your "Transition Walk" (the sticky notes that call out to you as important) and complete the strategic plan grid by identifying specific goals; forming the strategy that actualizes the goals; creating the action plan for each goal that includes the responsible person; outlining the outcome that the goal will produce; providing the timeline you plan to follow for implementation and completion; informing the status of your progress that is updated as you go; and initiating an evaluation of your learnings, success, or challenges. Here is the sample strategic plan grid as a guide:

Goal #1: Creating a Healthy Romantic Relationship

Strategy	Action Plan	Outcome	Timeline	Status	Evaluation
Create an understanding of the type of relationship I want to have ———— Understand the difference between healthy and unhealthy relationships ———— Develop a plan for seeking a healthy relationship and implement plan	I will work with a relationship coach to better understand (me in) relationships ———— I will research the difference between healthy and unhealthy relationships ———— I will implement my plan	I will have the healthy relationship of my dreams ———— I will be fulfilled in my healthy relationship	Meet with relationship coach by June 1, 2014 ———— Create plan by July 1, 2014 ———— Implement Plan by July 15, 2014 ———— Complete goal by December 31, 2014	I identified a coach and met my deadline ———— I am working on implementing my healthy relationship plan	Working with a coach to identify and understand healthy relationships, and my role in them, has helped me be more successful in relationship with self and others ———— I am enjoying my healthy relationship

You may want to consider the following questions as you complete this task: What came before that prepares you for this outcome and/or the goals you identified? What preparation is needed now? Where do you anticipate getting stuck? How do you get unstuck in order to move forward again? Is fear coming up and if so, how are you planning to use it as a guide to move forward? What or who is your support system? What Mindfulness Attitudes and/or ah-ha's from this book offer guidance for moving forward?

This strategic plan includes concrete action steps for you to actualize your desired life.

Materials Needed: Playdough, Journal, and Pen

To end our guidebook journey together, I invite you to participate, again, in an activity that will culminate our time together and gauge where you find yourself at this stage of creating your desire life. This activity is called: "Mold Me, Again". Open the canister of Playdough and complete these steps:

7. Using your Playdough, mold a representation of who you think you are in this moment.

8. Write in your journal what you created, what you think and feel about it, what ah-ha's (learnings) you discovered, and how this molding is different from the one you created in the introduction.

9. Now, mold with your Playdough, a representation of the "journey" you took using this guidebook towards your desired life.

10. Write in your journal what you created, what you think and feel about it, what ah-ha's you discovered, and how this molding is different from the one you created in the introduction.

11. Lastly, mold with your Playdough, a representation of the desired life as you now know it to be true.

12. Write in your journal what you created, what you think and feel about it, what ah-ha's you discovered, and how this molding is different from the one you created in the introduction.

It has been an honor and a privilege being a part of your journey. I wish you well as you move forward in creating and securing the life you desire. Please remember that life is a journey; destinations are moment-to-moment outcomes that create a full life of joy. I hope you found this guidebook helpful. It is a guidebook that can, and should, be revisited throughout your life, as you will continue to evolve and will find new information and activities that meet your needs in each moment.

This guidebook is a tool for you in your life. This guidebook is also a tool for me in my coaching and consulting practice. I am available for ongoing coaching and consulting if you found this useful, but want to explore its content in more depth and/or go to the next level. My website contains information about upcoming workshops and retreats and how to schedule coaching or consulting sessions. Coaching and consulting are available in person, by phone, or by other forms of electronic means. Visit me on the web at: www.catalysthealthysolutions.com.

"Go confidently in the directions of your dreams! Live the life you've imagined" (Henry David Thoreau). Be well as you journey on!

Journey Journal

Capture your story & ah-ha's here

_____

_____

_____

_____

_____

_____

_____

_____

_____

_____

_____

_____

_____

_____

_____

_____

Acknowledgments

This book was possible because of the love and support of my family, friends, and colleagues. It takes a community to build a book, and I am blessed to have you all as my community. My gratitude runs deep for the following reviewers and copyeditors who helped shape this book: Kellie Mitchell, Verna Lind, Melita Schwartz, Mark Schwartz, Jordana DeZeeuw Spencer, and Dan Spencer. Thank you to Taylor Ivey for assisting in the creation of the graphics and layout for the book – I love your creative ideas and spirit – and for helping with marketing. I want to thank my parents, Verna and Jerry, and my brother Mark for your unconditional love and unwavering support during all of the journeys of my life. It has been a crazy ride at times, but we have all weathered the storms with dignity and strength. I love you! Words cannot fully capture how much I love and cherish my wife, Melita, and our son Rowland. Melita, you have been my rock. You stand strong with me and for me and I am eternally grateful. It is an honor and privilege being your wife, co-parent, and business partner. Thank you for loving me through this journey and all the journeys we create together. I love you! Rowland, you are my dream come true. I never knew it possible to love someone so deeply – and here you are providing me the opportunity to love you so fully and to learn through your experiences in each and every moment. I wish for you endless journeys that create a wondrous and fulfilling desired life. I am happy beyond measure to be on this journey with you. I love you! Thank you to all of my colleagues and collaborators – you inspire greatness and make the world, and those in it, a little bit better each and every day. And lastly, I want to thank all of the clients, students, and participants with whom I have worked over the decades. Watching you valiantly journey to your desired life has been inspirational. I have learned with you and from you and have grown as a person and practitioner.

I am truly blessed!

Made in the USA
Columbia, SC
05 October 2018